PROBLEMS

of the

SPIRIT-FILLED

LIFE

Other Books by the Same Author

PROBLEMS

of the

SPIRIT-FILLED

LIFE

William S. Deal, Th.D.

Beacon Hill Press
Kansas City, Missouri

Preface

For several years the general theme of the material in this work was used for a series of lectures in camps and conventions where occasion arose or they were demanded. Almost without fail there has been considerable demand for these lectures in book form.

While pursuing graduate studies in theology it occurred to the writer that this field would afford an area of further research which would be suitable for a dissertation and which could also later be arranged for publication in book form. Upon submission of the program to the proper authorities permission was granted and the dissertation produced is here presented, with such revisions as were proper to prepare it for book form.

The book has been divided into four sections. This has been done in order to deal more specifically and at length with each of the major areas in which the most outstanding problems of everyday Spirit-filled living will be found.

The section on doctrine was thought very essential for those who may be for the first time being introduced to the teaching of the Spirit-filled experience and life, and especially for young people who should become better acquainted with this great doctrine. While not strictly a problem of Spirit-filled living, the doctrine is certainly very basic to its approach.

If slight repetitions occur, these arise from the nature of the matter under discussion being so closely connected with another similar point or phase of the over-all picture. The many quotations, some at considerable length, should prove invaluable to the younger reader, especially in acquainting him with some of the literature in this field.

The writer sincerely prays that this work shall prove a blessing to the reader in its perusal as it has been to him in its preparation.

WILLIAM S. DEAL

Acknowledgments

The following publishers have kindly granted permission to quote from their publications:

Abingdon Press, Nashville, Tennessee: *Adam Clarke's Commentary*, Volume VI, Adam Clarke.

William B. Eerdmans Publishing Company, Grand Rapids, Michigan: *Christian Theology*, P. B. Fitzwater, 1938; *Lectures in Systematic Theology*, H. C. Theissen, 1951; *Man in the Process of Time*, J. Stafford Wright.

Light and Life Press, Winona Lake, Indiana: *Foundations of Doctrine*, H. E. Jessop, 1938; *Three D's of the Sanctified*, F. Lincicome, 1932; *The Music of Pentecost*, J. Paul Taylor, 1945; *Blueprint for a Christian World*, Mary A. Tenney, 1953; *The More Excellent Way*, G. A. Turner, 1952.

Macmillan Company, New York, New York: *Abnormal Psychology*, Carney Landis and M. M. Bolles, 1949.

Metheun & Company, Publishers, London, England: *Psychology and Morals*, J. A. Hadfield, 1949.

Moody Press, Chicago, Illinois: *The Person and Work of the Holy Spirit*, Rene Pache, 1954; *Baptism with the Holy Spirit*, R. A. Torrey.

Pentecostal Publishing Company, Louisville, Kentucky: *Pastoral Sketches*, B. Carradine.

Fleming H. Revell Company, Westwood, New Jersey: *Lectures to Professing Christians*, Charles G. Finney, 1897.

Warner Press, Anderson, Indiana: *Deeper Experience of Famous Christians*, J. G. Lawson, 1911.

Wesley Press, Marion, Indiana: *The Holy Spirit*, J. A. Huffman, 1938.

West Publishing Company, Apollo, Pennsylvania: *Pentecostal Papers*, S. A. Keen, 1946.

Table of Contents

Introduction

This book, appropriately titled *Problems of the Spirit-filled Life,* is one of common and pressing interest to every conscientious Christian, young or old. It deals with the very fabric of life itself and comes to grips with the basic realities of the everyday pattern of Christian living. It is a realistic view of the godly life.

The ideals of holy living are brought well into focus by the author of this book, and the pattern of sainthood is defined clearly. The daily grind of temptation and pressures, as well as the releases of joyful experience in God, are set side by side in such a manner as to make daily Christian living an experience of determination and joy which will definitely bring maturity and establishment in divine grace.

The author has written a fine, practical message for the layman and has answered his problems well and with great simplicity. But on the other hand he has succeeded in presenting his material in such a fashion as to make a workbook for the classroom. The artful classroom instructor could use the text well as an introduction to practical theology and the philosophy of daily living. It would fit well the demands of collateral reading and research.

I have known the author, Dr. William S. Deal, for many years. The book reflects the man, and as such reflects the New Testament experience of divine grace.

R. D. GUNSALUS, D.D.
President, Eastern Pilgrim College

Section One

Doctrine of the Holy Spirit

But the Comforter, which is the Holy Ghost, whom the Father will send in my name, he shall teach you all things, and bring all things to your remembrance, whatsoever I have said unto you (John 14:26).

But when the Comforter is come, whom I will send unto you from the Father, even the Spirit of truth, which proceedeth from the Father, he shall testify of me: and ye also shall bear witness, because ye have been with me from the beginning (John 15:26-27).

Howbeit when he, the Spirit of truth, is come, he will guide you into all truth: for he shall not speak of himself; but whatsoever he shall hear, that shall he speak: and he will shew you things to come (John 16:13).

CHAPTER I

Personality of the Holy Spirit

No study of the problems connected with the Spirit-filled life can properly avoid in its beginning an examination of the *definitions* of the several matters concerning the personality of the Holy Spirit, His offices and work in this dispensation; and something of the doctrine of sanctification, correct terminology in expressing this doctrine, and provisions for proper candidates for this experience.

This is the dispensation of the Holy Spirit, and His administration is naturally very prominent upon the pages of the New Testament. In every experiential relationship to God and in all the various problems associated with the Spirit-filled life, the Holy Spirit plays so prominent a role that one cannot escape attention to His place in such living. One has well said, "The Holy Ghost represents God to us in our own hearts, and spirits, and consciences . . . who, when His closest communion with man is described, can only be described as the Spirit pleading with him, or dwelling with him." [1]

That the Holy Spirit is a Personality is abundantly clear from the Scriptures, especially in the New Testament. Let us note very concisely the major evidences of the personality of the Holy Spirit.

Definition of Personality. Of the basic elements of personality Dr. Huffman has said: "Of these there are three: the intellect, the sensibility, and the will. These three God-given powers, which we may call soul powers, every normal individual possesses and exhibits. They form a complex, threefold in character, and cannot be reduced to less. Every functioning which can be predicated of any intelligent, human being can be catalogued under one of these three powers."[2] Fitzwater states it well: "By personality is meant separateness of being, individuality, mode of subsistence. The essential characteristics of a personality are self-consciousness, emotion and self-will. All beings lacking these attributes are not persons."[3]

Personality Characteristics. Many of these are applied to the Holy Spirit in Scripture by which His personality is established. Thiessen has pointed out that "personal pronouns are used of Him, (John 14:17; 16:13) . . . Again we prove His personality by the name Comforter. The term occurs only in John 14:16, 26; 15:26; 16:7 and refers to the Holy Spirit. It is applied to Christ in John 14:16; I John 2:1 (Greek); and since it expresses personality when applied to Christ, it must do so also when applied to the Spirit."[4]

Furthermore, personal characteristics ascribed to Him add to the evidence. The three essential elements of personality are so ascribed: intellect (I Cor. 2:11); sensibility (Rom. 8:27; 15:30); and will (I Cor. 12:11).

Again, by the works ascribed to Him we prove His personality. He works (I Cor. 12:11), searches (I Cor. 2:10), speaks (Acts 13:2), testifies (John 15:26), teaches (John 14:26), reproves (John 16:8-11), regenerates (John 3:5), prays (Rom. 8:26), guides into truth (John 16:13), glorifies Christ (John 16:14), calls men into service (Acts 13:2), and directs them in service (Acts 16:6-7).

His personality is further established by His association with the Father and the Son, as in the baptismal formula spoken by Christ (Matt. 28:19); in the apostolic benediction by St. Paul (II Cor. 13:14); and in His office as Administrator of the Church (I Cor. 12:4-6).

Finally, we may prove His personality by His susceptibility to personal treatment as seen in the fact that

He may be tempted (Acts 5:9), lied to (Acts 5:3), grieved (Eph. 4:30; Isa. 63:10), resisted (Acts 7:51), insulted (Heb. 10:29), and blasphemed (Matt. 12:31-32).

That the Holy Spirit is very and eternal God, with the Father and the Son, may be seen from His association with them in His works. Huffman has listed these as follows: creation (Gen. 1:1-2; John 1:1, 3, 10), inspiration of the scriptures (Heb. 1:1; I Pet. 1:10-11; II Peter 1:21), redemption (I John 4:14; I Tim. 2:6; John 16:7-8). Fitting His deity likewise is the ascription to Him of divine attributes, such as: eternity (Heb. 9:14), omnipotence (Luke 1:35; Rom. 15:18-19), omnipresence (Ps. 139:7-8), omniscience (I Cor. 2:10-11), dispensing of wisdom and knowledge (I Cor. 12:8). Seven works of Deity are also ascribed to Him: the generation of Jesus (Luke 1:35), the anointing of Jesus (Matt. 3:16), the filling and guidance of Jesus (Luke 4:1), the resurrection of Jesus (I Pet. 3:18), the regeneration of man (John 3:5), the sanctification of man (Rom. 15:16), the resurrection of man (Rom. 8:11).[5]

Offices and Gifts of the Holy Spirit. Further proof of the Holy Spirit's personality may be seen in His relationship to the redemptive work of God. There have been only three great dispensations; however many divisions may be made within them by Bible scholars. These have been the Dispensation of the Father, from the creation to the birth of Christ, or the opening of His ministry; the Dispensation of the Son, from His birth or baptism to Calvary or perhaps Pentecost; and the Dispensation of the Holy Spirit, from Pentecost to the end of this age.[6] We are now in the Dispensation of the Holy Spirit; hence, He is the Executive of the Trinity in this age. As Huffman says: "Since the Holy Spirit is the successor of Christ, he should be recognized as the only duly qualified administrator of the affairs of grace in this dispensation."[7]

As God the Father was the Administrator of the old covenant of promises and law, and as Christ the Son has instituted the new covenant of His blood by which free grace has come to all, the Holy Spirit has been by the Father and Son placed in charge as the Administrator of this new covenant for this age. This is what is commonly meant when we refer to the "office" of the Holy Spirit. He is the Administrator of grace and the Dispenser of gifts to man during this dispensation. Our Saviour states something of the work of the Holy Spirit. "And when he is come, he will reprove the world of sin, and of righteousness, and of judgment: of sin, because they believe not on me; of righteousness, because I go to my Father, and ye see me no more; of judgment, because the prince of this world is judged." He convicts of sin and regenerates penitents; reveals the righteousness of Christ to men and works it out in them; and warns the impenitent of coming judgment with no uncertain means, such as the Word, conscience, and providence.

The "gifts" of the Spirit are dealt with more largely in I Corinthians 12 and Ephesians 4:11-14 than anywhere else in the New Testament. In these passages the gifts of apostleship, prophetic office, evangelist, pastor, and teacher are set forth as the instructional gifts. Healing, faith, and miracles may be listed as miraculous gifts; helps and governments, as relief and administration; and tongues and interpretation of tongues, as the ecstatic. This grouping by Huffman follows Jamieson, Fausset, and Brown's *Commentary*.[8] It is not our purpose to enlarge upon these gifts but merely to list them as part of the Holy Spirit's official relationship to the Church and a further evidence of His personality.

Here we rest our case, as it is hardly necessary to produce further evidence of the personality of the Holy Spirit for a work of this limited scope.

We turn now to a brief survey of the controversy that raged in the Early Church concerning the doctrine of the Holy Spirit. The nature of this work would forbid any prolonged discussion or historical review of the matter to be considered. It is felt, however, that a few notes respecting this matter may be profitably added here.

Until the latter part of the third century A.D., the personality of the Holy Spirit was never seriously questioned. There were here and there a few writers who made inferences in question of the deity and personality of the Holy Spirit, but they were not of sufficient authority to warrant any attention by the Church. "In the primitive creeds," says one authority, "belief in the Holy Spirit was professed in a distinct article, whose parallel structure to the articles on the Father and Son indicates the essential place of the Holy Spirit in the Trinity."[9] The Holy Spirit's relation to the Church in the preservation of its unity, inspiration of its sacred writings, the guidance into truth, the forgiveness of sins, and the resurrection of the body was held as sacred as in the formative days of the apostles themselves by the Church at large.

During the latter part of the third century and the early years of the fourth, however, there arose a heretical movement known in church history as Arianism. Its chief promoter was Arius, a presbyter of Alexandria, of whom little is known as to his early years. He adopted the doctrine of Lucian of Antioch that Christ was created by the Father in the prehistoric eternities and came to earth as the "logos," sort of second essence of God, and took upon himself a human body. He was, then, neither perfect God nor perfect man. From this heresy grew the notion that the Holy Spirit was a mere "creature," also created by God. While His deity was thus denied, His personality was at first upheld and He was assigned a place similar to "ministering angels," only far more exalted.

This heresy was first condemned officially by the Council of Nicaea in A.D. 325. It continued to work havoc in the Church, especially the Eastern church, however, until much later. It was again condemned by the Synod of Alexandria which demanded that all who would receive Holy Communion must condemn "those who say that the Holy Spirit is a creature and separate from the substance of Christ." The deity of Christ had been reaffirmed by the Council of Nicaea in A.D. 325, when He was declared to be of "one substance with the Father." Leading church fathers defended the doctrine of the Holy Spirit, among whom were Athanasius, one of the greatest characters of the Early Church, and Basil of Caesarea. The emperors Constantius and Theodosius the Great likewise used their political powers to help quell the heresy.

Finally, the Council of Constantinople in 381 dealt a deathblow to Arianism and its claims. The Nicene-Constantinople Creed, most likely the work of this council, sets forth the doctrine of the Holy Spirit thus: "[We believe] in the Holy Spirit, the Lord, the giver of life, who proceeds from the Father, who with the Father and the Son is together worshipped and glorified, who spoke through the prophets."[10] With this crushing defeat Arianism, while far from ceasing to trouble the Church, nevertheless began to die away and in the following centuries had no official following.

Arianism has never entirely perished, however, in some form. Some modern liberal theological writers still insist that the term Holy Spirit is merely a personification of religious experience. Just as sin, the law, justice, etc. are sometimes personified in relation to human experience, so they would make St. Paul and St. John merely personify the Holy Spirit as an expression of Christian experience in relation to God's expression of His love and grace to and in themselves. This view is equally as erroneous as Arianism. It not only denies the deity of the Holy Spirit but His personality as well. It leaves Him only as a divine influence, an emanation or projection of God into human religious experience. This all orthodox Protestantism rejects and condemns as heresy.

The great body of the Church has ever maintained the doctrine of the personality of the Holy Spirit throughout the Christian centuries. This truth is perhaps more widely accepted today than at any time since the rise of modern liberalism.

With this truth firmly established in our thinking let us turn to the next important phase of our study.

CHAPTER II

Provisions for
the Spirit-filled Life

The Holy Spirit is the Regenerator of the repentant, believing sinner.[11] Likewise He is the Sanctifier of the believer who fully trusts in Christ for deliverance from sin. It is His office to apply the blood of the Saviour to the believer's need, and to guide, teach, comfort, and sustain him in his every experience of life.

Reference to the great creeds of the Church will prove that all believers have accepted the fact that sanctification is part of the doctrine and experience of the Christian life. But there have been considerable diversities of opinion as to what constitutes this experience, when it is received, and whether or not it is instantaneous or gradual, a crisis experience or one extending over a lifetime. Examination of the works upon this important subject will reveal that most theologians accept the fact that sanctification is subsequent to regeneration and that it is an experience continuing throughout a lifetime. The major division has come at the point of whether or not entire sanctification is a crisis experienced by the believer by which he is "cleansed from all sin" and made perfect in love. Such writers as Biederwolf, Torrey, and Cumming even maintained that sanctification, or rather as they termed it, "the baptism with the Holy Spirit," was a crisis experience, but they denied that it was accompanied by or accomplished in the believer a cleansing from all sin.[12] They maintained that it gave power over sin so that it may be restrained by the believer from expressing itself so that he may live what was called by them "the victorious life." This way of life, they taught, will become more and more in harmony with the Saviour's teaching and the New Testament admonitions by a progressive sanctification.

On the other hand, John Wesley and his followers have taught instantaneous sanctification accomplished by a crisis in the believer's heart by faith in Christ as he accepts the finished work of the Saviour to be efficacious to cleanse from all sin and to make the heart perfect in love before God. This experience they maintain may be had in an instant of time and carried on throughout life unto the end. They do, however, also teach gradual sanctification. This they believe precedes "entire sanctification," so termed by Mr. Wesley, and in some sense may also follow the crisis experience. By this gradual sanctification is meant a dedication to the Lord and a giving of one's self more fully to Him until one reaches that point or place in his experience where he may by faith lay hold of God for full sanctification. After this crisis experience it may consist in a growth in grace by which a more complete giving of one's ransomed powers to God in service and a deeper sense of His love may be developed in the believer's heart and life.

As Binney and Steele have pointed out,[13] this doctrine of immediate sanctification is supported by an abundance of scripture passages:

1. *It is the will of God.* This is abundantly proved by such references as John 17:17; Rom. 12:1-2; Eph. 5:17-18; Col. 4:12; I Thess. 4:3, 7-8; and Heb. 10:9-10.

2. *It is the command of God.* This may be seen from Gen. 17:1; Exod. 19:6; Lev. 11:44; Deut. 6:5; Matt. 5:48; 22:37; John 5:14; Rom. 12:1-2; II Cor. 7:1; Heb. 6:1; Jas. 1:4; and I Pet. 1:15-16.

3. *It is promised by God.* This may be seen in Ps. 119:1-3; Isa. 1:18; Jer. 33:8; John 7:38-39; Heb. 7:25; 10:16-25; I John 1:7, 9.

4. *It is revealed in the experience sought by prayer.*
Ps. 51:2, 7, 9; Hos. 14:2; Matt. 6:10; John 17:17; and
I Thess. 5:23-24.

5. *It is seen in the examples recorded in the lives
of people.* Gen. 6:8-9; II Kings 20:3; 23:25; Job 1:1, 22;
Ps. 37:37; Luke 1:67; I Cor. 2:6; Phil. 3:15; I Thess. 2:10;
and Heb. 12:23.

We deem this to be sufficient to illustrate the scriptural provisions for the Spirit-filled life. There are, however, many other references which point to this as God's
will and provision for His people. The story of Pentecost
and of Cornelius' household and of the Ephesian con-
verts further illustrates this truth as listed by Luke in
Acts, chapters 2, 10, 11, and 19. Jesus promised His
disciples that the Holy Spirit would be given to them
(John 14:15-18; 14:25-26; 15:26-27; 16:7-15); and St.
Paul exhorted the Ephesians to "be filled with the
Spirit" (5:18), which we may suppose was a standard
exhortation to all Christians.

Let us now return to a more full explanation of this
"instantaneous sanctification" as taught by John Wesley
and those since his day who believe this to be the scriptural teaching concerning God's will for believers. Mr.
Wesley says:

> We are all agreed, we may be saved from all sin be-
> fore death; that is, from all sinful tempers and desires . . .
> But as to the circumstances, is the change gradual or
> instantaneous? It is both the one and the other. "But
> should we in preaching insist both on one and the
> other?" Certainly we should insist on the gradual change;
> and that earnestly and continually. And are there not
> reasons why we should insist on the instantaneous change?
> If there be such a blessed change before death, should
> we not encourage all believers to expect it? . . . They
> are saved by hope, by this hope of a total change, with
> a gradually increasing salvation. Destroy this hope, and
> that salvation stands still, or rather decreases daily;

therefore, whoever would advance the grandual change in believers should strongly insist on the instantaneous.[14]

Christian perfection was the term quite largely used by Wesley and the early Methodists, although they frequently also spoke of the experience as "entire sanctification." Of this experience Wesley says:

What is Christian perfection?
The loving of God with all our heart, mind, soul and strength. This implies that no wrong temper, none contrary to love, remains in the soul; and that all the thoughts, words, and actions are governed by pure love.[15]

We shall submit one more question from Wesley in which he illustrates his meaning of gradual and instantaneous sanctification. In response to the question, "Is this death to sin and renewal in love gradual or instantaneous?" he replies:

A man may be dying for some time, yet he does not, properly speaking, die to the instant the soul is separated from the body; and in that instant he lives the life of eternity. In like manner he may be dying to sin for some time, yet he is not dead to sin till sin is separated from his soul; and in that instant he lives the full life of love. And as the change undergone when the body dies is of a different kind, and infinitely greater than any we had known before, yea, such as till then it is impossible to conceive; so the change wrought when the soul dies to sin is of a different kind, and infinitely greater than any before, and than any can conceive till he experiences it. Yet he still grows in grace and in the knowledge of Christ, in the love and image of God, and will do so, not only till death, but probably to all eternity.[16]

For those who are not acquainted with the doctrine of entire sanctification, we would recommend Wesley's *Plain Account of Christian Perfection*. Upon this statement of doctrine the great Methodist church and those since her founding embracing hre peculiar doctrine of

Christian perfection have rested their faith. It is a brief but very clear statement to which little need be added.

Bishop Peck of the Methodist church maintained that this doctrine of sanctification was the "central idea of Christianity." He said of it:

> Holiness is not an outside or accidental appendage of Christianity. It is the very center of it—the grand element of its power—the essential fact of its value . . . The central idea which has produced revelation has filled it with counsels which "he that runs may read," and which followed in the spirit of humble confidence, will surely lead us to the full realization of this glorious state.[17]

Commissioner Brengle of the Salvation Army once described the experience of sanctification as follows:

> Do you want to know what Holiness is? It is *pure* love. Do you want to know what the Baptism of the Holy Ghost is? It is not mere sentiment. It is not a happy sensation that passes away in a night. It is a baptism of love that brings every thought into captivity to the Lord Jesus; that casts out all fear; that burns up doubt and unbelief as fire burns tow; that makes one "meek and lowly in heart;" that makes one hate uncleanness, lying and deceit, a flattering tongue, and every evil way with a perfect hatred; that makes Heaven and Hell eternal realities; that makes one patient and gentle with the froward and sinful; that makes one "pure, peaceable, easy to be intreated, full of mercy and good fruits, without partiality and without hypocrisy;" that brings one into perfect and unbroken sympathy with the Lord Jesus Christ in His toil and travail to bring a lost and rebel world back to God.[18]

We believe these references sufficiently define the doctrine and experience of entire sanctification for this present work. They clearly express the Wesleyan position upon the matter of deliverance from sin in this life, by the grace of God, through Jesus Christ our Lord, and emphasize that adequate provision has been made for the believer's cleansing and that this fact is attested by Scripture.

Chapter III

Proper Terminology

It may be well here to state briefly the terms by which this experience of sanctification is often identified, both in Scripture and the literature upon this subject. Binney and Steele have well stated the general terms used and given an over-all definition:

> This state is variously expressed in the scriptures, so that we need not be tenacious of any particular phrase by which to designate it. It is called *holiness, sanctification, purity, perfection, fullness of God,* and *of Christ,* and of the *Holy Ghost,* and *full assurance of faith.* What is meant by these expressions is, that participation of the Divine nature which excludes all original depravity or inbred sin from the heart, and fills it with perfect love to God and man—perfect love, the unction of the Holy One, and the baptism of the Holy Ghost.[19]

A more correct usage of the proper terminology would serve to clarify what is the proper function and state of the experience with reference to its application to the believer and the resultant life following. One of the strongest scriptural terms for sanctification in the Wesleyan interpretation is not even used in this classification by Binney and Steele, for example. It is the term "cleansing from all sin," as noted by John in his First Epistle (I John 1:7-9). Let us note the special significance of several of these terms as they relate to the experience and life of the believer.

The root word in the Greek from which our word sanctify comes (*hagiadzo*), means "to separate, consecrate; cleanse, purify, sanctify; regard or reverence as holy."[20] It may be seen at once that the meaning of the word must be judged by its context and its usage in the text in which it appears. Two examples are John 17:19, "And for their sakes I sanctify myself, that they also might be sanctified through the truth"; and I Thess. 5:23, "And the very God of peace sanctify you wholly . . ." In the first instance the Saviour refers to himself, in connection with which another reference may be quoted—"whom the Father hath sanctified, and sent into the world." These usages of the word must signify to separate and dedicate to a holy purpose or usage, as Christ had no sin from which to be made pure. In the last reference of Paul to the Thessalonians the word evidently means a cleansing from sin or to make pure, since he prays to God to do the sanctifying of these people. The Thessalonians could dedicate and consecrate themselves but the purifying must be done by the Lord; nor would the Lord "consecrate" them, since this was the human side of the work which they would need to perform. In general New Testament usage, where believers are referred to as being sanctified or exhorted to be sanctified, sanctification is a work to be performed by themselves in consecrating themselves to God, and by God in cleansing them from sin. This is the meaning of the term as used by most writers who follow the Wesleyan interpretation. This is the "experience" or crisis of Christian perfection, and is the same thing as being "cleansed from all sin," as being "dead indeed unto sin," a result of the cleansing, and as "being made perfect in love."

It should here be pointed out that, while sanctification is the experience of the believer, it is the blood of Christ which is the efficacious *means* by which this is accomplished (I John 1:7, 9).

Holiness or heart purity is the *state* in which the believer lives after he has been cleansed from sin. It is therefore not correct to say, *"I received holiness when Christ cleansed my heart."* Sanctification is a work, partly progressive but finally instantaneous, while holiness is the state or condition which results from the believer's being cleansed. So likewise are "the full assurance of faith," the "fulness of God," and similar expressions referring to the state after full sanctification.

The Holy Spirit is the sanctifying Agent who applies the blood of Christ for the believer's cleansing. Based upon the fact of the shed Blood being meritorious to atone for the inward sin and pollution of the believer's heart, the Spirit works in him the change which we know as sanctification or cleansing. This is always upon conditions which the believer must meet.

The baptism with the Holy Ghost, then, while amounting to the same thing experientially as sanctification, is nevertheless essentially an operation of the Spirit upon the believer by which sanctification is accomplished. This may be seen by the reference, "that the offering up of the Gentiles might be acceptable, being sanctified by the Holy Ghost" (Rom. 15:16).

John the Baptist associated "fire" with this baptism of the Holy Spirit (Matt. 3:11), and Luke reports that there were "tongues like as of fire" accompanying the Pentecostal baptism with the Holy Spirit (Acts 2:3). Now fire is a purifying agent and its association with this baptism is highly significant of the fact that this baptism of the believer with the Holy Spirit is accompanied by a cleansing of the believer's heart. This should be clearly apparent to those who have been accustomed to think of it as a baptism of power for *suppressing* inward sin in the believer, as well as those who think of it as a post-sanctification experience for life and power. There is apparently no New Testament teaching which separates the baptism with the Holy Spirit from the cleansing from sin of the believer. There are references where cleansing is not associated with it by direct reference to it, such as John 7:38-39, where life-giving water is the figure employed, and the case of the Ephesian Christians (Acts 19:1-6). However, the baptism of the Holy Spirit upon the house of Cornelius is said to have been directly connected with cleansing," . . . giving them the Holy Ghost

... purifying their hearts by faith" (Acts 15:8-9). It is furthermore stated that God gave them the Holy Spirit as He did the disciples at Pentecost (verse 8), which signifies (if language can be made to mean anything at all) that there was a purification of the disciples' hearts at Pentecost.

Not only is the Holy Spirit the sanctifying Agent of the believer, but He is the constantly abiding Comforter, Teacher, and Guide of the believer. The word rendered "Comforter" has been rendered "Paraclete" sometimes, and once is rendered "advocate" (I John 2:1), referring to Christ in His Mediatorial work. The Greek form is *paraklatos: para*—"alongside"; *klatos*—"to call." Hence, one called alongside to assist another. References are John 14:16, 26; 15:26; 16:7.

It was Biederwolf's opinion that the word Advocate is much more expressive and should have been used throughout where the word Comforter appears. Certainly Paraclete would have been better than Comforter, as the latter suggests but one meaning of the original—to comfort —whereas the original really carries the ideas of defense, assistance, and help as well as comfort. The term Advocate also accords with the Greek usage where the friend or relative of one in trouble stood before the judge to plead his cause, or sometimes an agent of the party pleaded the case. It appears that Advocate more nearly expresses what Jesus and John had in mind in the references above.[21]

By the term "Christian perfection" generally two things are meant. Primarily, it is intended to express that perfection of love to God and our fellow men which the sanctifying grace of Christ imparts to our hearts. There is no such thing as human perfection now; nor may mankind attain unto angelic perfection, even in eternity. To love God with all the heart, mind, soul, and strength is all that God or man could require of one. But there is a secondary meaning which attaches to this idea also. It is that of Christian maturity. The original from which the word "perfect" in Matt. 5:48 is rendered means "absolutely finished." So likewise Heb. 6:1 suggests a perfection of maturity. Christian perfection should reap its best fruits in growth and maturity of those whose hearts have been made pure by this experience. The quality of divine love could not be changed in an eternity, but the quantity of it may progress on and on forever. And this increase in quantity is what makes for spiritual development and maturation of Christians in outward conduct and character.

If everyone would be careful to use the proper terms in describing this wonderful experience of grace, much confusion and misunderstanding could be avoided.

CHAPTER IV

Proper Candidates

Mr. Wesley in his *Plain Account of Christian Perfection* makes it abundantly clear that only regenerated believers are candidates for this experience.[22] Numerous references in the New Testament to the baptism with the Holy Spirit or His coming to the disciples indicate that this experience was to be post-regenerative. In Luke 10:20, Jesus exhorted His disciples to rejoice, not in the fact that demons were subject to them in their ministry, "but rather rejoice, because your names are written in heaven." This accords with the reference to the saints' having their names written in the "Lamb's book of life," and evidently means to signify to us that these men were considered children of God even then, a considerable while before Pentecost. In John 17:14, Jesus, praying to the Father, said of His disciples, "They are not of the world, even as I am not of the world." And again, "None of them is lost, but the son of perdition" (v. 12). In verse 8 He declared that they had believed on Him, which John 1:12 connects directly with salvation. So then, as John 7:38-39 points out, the Holy Spirit was to be given to them that believe, and the disciples as believers were candidates, which Pentecost translated into reality. If "God is no respecter of persons," it still remains that believers today are candidates for the baptism with the Holy Spirit. Some point out that this was before Pentecost, and maintain that since Pentecost all men receive the baptism with the Spirit at regeneration. But this cannot be scripturally maintained. And indeed such men as Moody, Torrey, Biederwolf, Cumming, and Billy Graham today, while not believing that the baptism with the Holy Spirit brings cleansing from all sin in sanctifying grace, yet have maintained that it is a crisis experience, subsequent to regeneration.[23]

Mr. Wesley declared that in his day there were many witnesses to this grace. It is noted that there were between three and four hundred in the London society who professed to have been made perfect in love. In more recent times a great multitude of God's people around the world have thus witnessed to full cleansing from sin and the abiding presence of the Holy Spirit, and they consistently proclaim that this experience came to them after their regeneration.

Section Two

Differences of the Spirit-filled Life

For one believeth that he may eat all things: another, who is weak, eateth herbs. Let not him that eateth despise him that eateth not; and let not him which eateth not judge him that eateth: for God hath received him (Rom. 14: 2-3).

Now there are diversities of gifts, but the same Spirit. And there are differences of administrations, but the same Lord. And there are diversities of operations, but it is the same God which worketh all in all. But the manifestation of the Spirit is given to every man to profit withal (I Cor. 12: 4-7).

CHAPTER V

Differences in Approach

As there are no two human beings physically and emotionally alike, so there are no two Christian experiences alike. There are similarities in all persons which identify them as members of a certain family or race, and there are likewise similarities in the Christian experiences of regeneration and sanctification by which they may be identified. There is an over-all pattern which is always consistent in the experiences of all Spirit-filled believers, but there is no uniformity as to the details.

The endeavor to press for uniformity of details in this experience has led to a thousand confusions and disappointments and has sometimes so discouraged believers as to cause them to give up hope of obtaining the experience. In some cases believers who have obtained this experience have been perplexed by doubts because of this confusion when under heavy pressure from the enemy. Unwise advice or public teaching along this line has also been a hindrance. For instance, pressing for either of two extremes, overflowing joy or a deep sense of self-crucifixion in the believer at the time of his sanctification, can become a matter of confusion to one not established in the knowledge of the truth about the experience. Both phases of the emotional reaction are proper, but the stressing of the one to the exclusion of the other is always unwise.

It is our purpose to examine some of the *differences* which accompany both the crisis experience and the afterlife of the Spirit-filled believer.

In *approaching* this experience there are many and varied differences. Some persons who have had more light concerning it will of necessity react differently both in seeking and in the emotional responses following it than those with less light. No definite method is taught in the New Testament as to how one is to seek either regeneration or the Spirit's fullness. We should therefore be cautious in our outlining such methods. At Pentecost no word is given as to the mode. The disciples may have been praying, singing, or meditating; however, "sitting" is the physical position noted in Acts 2:2. But they did not so remain long, for they were so soon out witnessing to the multitudes. Cornelius' household were most likely sitting in meditative attention when the Spirit descended upon them. Of the Ephesian disciples nothing is known except that they were most certainly in a receptive mood. Is it possible that we have over-emphasized the mode and underemphasized the faith of the seeking believer?

There are some persons whose light has been limited as to the condition of the "carnal heart" but whose hunger has been great for all the fullness of God so far as they understood it, whose approach to the experience has been characterized by a deep sense of joy. They have been quick to respond to the invitation to be "filled with the Spirit." Their faith has leaped up to receive the blessing and they have been filled with the joy of it without experiencing the deeper sense of pain and self-crucifixion which others have in their seeking. Some are quick to characterize such persons as having just received "a blessing" but not the fullness of sanctification. But is this a just criticism? Did not the believer so baptized obey "from the heart that form of doctrine which was delivered" unto him? Did he not "walk in the light, as he is in the light" in believing that God for Christ's sake did cleanse his heart and fill him with the Spirit? Am I therefore to become his judge even before I have seen the fruits of his experience under test? Is it truly Christian to cast doubt upon his experience if his life shows the fruits of "love, joy, peace, long-suffering, gentleness, goodness, faith, meekness, temperance" (Gal. 5:22-23), just because he did not "groan after the experience" as another might have done? It is doubtful whether such questions are of value to anyone, least of all to the questioner.

On the other hand, those who have had considerable light concerning the inward state of the carnal heart of the believer and yet have been dilatory to seek and obtain the experience of heart purity will sometimes suffer even a deeper sense of conviction for heart purity than they did for regeneration. They approach the experience with a deep sense of inward need. This brings them to "confess the sore plague of their heart," to experience self-searchings and self-crucifixion in endeavoring to bring themselves into a place of true faith for complete sanctification. Sometimes such persons experience a deep sense of quiet joy hardly to be compared to the hilarity which accompanied the experience of the person who came into it with less light and therefore less self-mortification. Nor can these latter persons be referred to as slow of heart, cold and indifferent to believe. Often this is not the case. Some, like John Fletcher of early Methodist fame, think of the experience as being so high and holy that they can scarcely attain unto it; or fear that once having obtained it they, like he, may lose it.

The approach to the experience is very gradual for some while it is much more progressive for others. The difference may be due to a number of causes. One is quick to perceive anything, the other slower. One may have a background which has been so out of harmony with the doctrine that he is hindered in seeking the experience thereby, even though his heart may hunger for the satisfaction described by those who have obtained it. The unknown factor must not be overlooked. In some cases persons could not stand a revelation of all God's demands upon them as readily as others. To the disciples Jesus said, "I have yet many things to say unto you, but ye cannot bear them now" (John 16:12). Reference to Mr. Wesley's *Plain Account of Christian Perfection* will suffice to show that he believed most persons who were made perfect in love reached that state by a gradual experience, ultimately climaxing in a crisis.[1]

Chapter VI

Differences in Receptivity

The difference in the reception of this experience is largely fixed by the differences in personalities and the amount of light and teaching one has had. Lincicome has pointed out that:

> No two are saved alike, no two are sanctified alike, and no two manifest it alike. Some will be noisy in manifesting what they feel, while others will be quiet.[2]

The extrovert personality will most likely have an explosive reaction to the Spirit's filling, crying aloud or rejoicing with a bubbling overflow. The introvert will normally respond much less emotionally so far as outward show is concerned. This pattern will likely continue in the lives of such persons throughout their lives. There are exceptions where the extrovert becomes more calm and self-possessed and the introvert is drawn out of his inner shell and becomes more expressive. Proper cultivation of personality traits to overcome the more undesirable ones and develop the better ones may result in such changes. But basically there will likely remain the more prominent characteristics of one's personality throughout life irrespective of training and development. For this reason one should not despise his essential personality traits but endeavor to understand himself and to develop himself to the best of his ability so that he may adapt himself to life's experiences and situations in such a way as to contribute the most to life and also get the best out of it.

Chapter VII

Differences in Emotional Reactions

As there are no two personalities alike, there are naturally no two persons whose emotional reactions are alike in every respect. While one who is known to have extroversive tendencies may receive the experience of sanctification with an outburst of joy, another with similar tendencies may nevertheless give vent to a flood of tears at the time the Spirit comes to him in His fullness. The same person will not always exhibit emotion alike under similar conditions. One may respond to the preaching of truth with joy at one time, with fear at another, and with a deep sense of unworthiness bordering upon depression at another time. The person who is thought of as an extrovert may likewise vary widely in his emotional responses to both the experience and the other religious stimuli afterward. He may even break out of his accustomed pattern of reaction and becomes very expressive of his emotions temporarily. It is sometimes the case that such a person once tasting the freedom of larger expression clings to it and becomes much freer in his testimony and other responses to outward demonstration. And there are also cases of persons suffering from extroversive tendencies who in striving to get away from them become excessively expressive of their emotions. Such persons at times have to watch against an almost fanatical extreme of exploding emotions. Others suffer much inwardly because they cannot bring themselves to such outward expressions of their emotions. They imagine if they could shout as someone else does this would be the height of glory for them. If they should try it they may find it not as happy an experiment as they had imagined. When one's spirit wells up with inward joy and the shout of praise literally mounts to his lips freely he will have no difficulty in expressing it. On the other hand, there are those who feel that if they could enjoy the rapturous quietness of some of their friends, instead of the boisterous nature they possess, they would find this exceeding bliss. But with this quietness they would soon find themselves quite as unsatisfied as they now think they are with their boisterousness at times. The better thing for each one to do is to learn to live with himself successfully and to control his emotions and direct them into the most successful channels of expression.

Emotional manifestations are likewise of a differing nature from person to person and from time to time in the same person. One cannot maintain an even poise at all times, never wavering emotionally to the right or the left. Even an ambivert with his very even disposition will sometimes vary in his emotional manifestations.

Something may be said also concerning the trials of persons relative to their emotional manifestations. There is an old story to the effect that two good ladies in the same church had a great trial over each other's manifestations in the services. Said Satan to one of them, "If you were a happy person like Mrs. Smith, joyously telling of your experiences with Christ in the services, people would have far more confidence in your religion." To Mrs. Brown he suggested, "Now look at yourself. You are always up in church telling of your experiences with laughter and gusto. People think you are just a big hypocrite. If you were only placid and quiet like Mrs. Smith and enjoyed the calm which her face mirrors, people would think you are truly a saint." Finally under this pressure the two good sisters decided to talk matters over with each other. Upon relating their experiences they discovered that each had a peculiar trial of her own. It is often the trick of Satan to tempt one to think of his own lot as not as satisfactory as that of another.

One must at all times remember that emotional manifestations have little or nothing to do with the matter of heart purity. They are largely controlled by one's psychological make-up and often by the circumstances which may at the time be playing upon the emotions. Sometimes one may experience a sinking of the emotions for no apparent reason, but this no more means that one has lost spiritual ground than that a slight indigestion indicates cancer of the stomach.

Keen has well said, "When the Holy Ghost is come, He tempers our high metal, disposes us to moderation, incites us to sweet allowances, restrains us from haste. The gift of the Holy Ghost does not destroy the heroic, but imparts the heavenly qualities of character."[3] The inward reign of the Holy Spirit, while not changing the essential personality, does help one to temper and control personality traits which might otherwise become a hindrance to his spiritual progress. Sometimes under the leadership of the Spirit the high-strung person slows down a bit and the slow one perks up some.

CHAPTER VIII

Differences in Aesthetic Appreciation

God made all of nature's beauties and evidently intended for them to be enjoyed by His creatures. Because of the great variety of human personalities He has made almost an infinite variety in objects of beauty. These beauties take many turns of fancy in the minds of as many different people. One extreme may be illustrated by the man who once told of how a fierce thunderstorm with its rolling black clouds was to him the most beautiful sight to behold. To many such a sight strikes terror to the mind.

One has difficulty in this age of appreciation for the beautiful of understanding how a brilliant mind like that of St. Augustine could have considered the enjoyment of the beautiful to be sinful. Baldwin summarizes from his *Confessions*, Book X, some of his ideas of what constituted sin in things of everyday life:

> (1) Impure dreams are a sign of a corrupt heart. (2) He considers pleasure in the taking of food a sin, saying, "This much hast Thou (God) taught me, that I should bring myself to take food as a medicine." (3) He considers that love for music is a sin. (4) He considers that it is a sin that "the eyes delight in fair and varied forms, and bright pleasing colors. (5) He considers it a sin to watch a hound chase a rabbit, a lizard or a spider catching flies, because this is prompted by curiosity, which, according to the theology of Augustine, is always evil.[4]

It is apparent that Augustine in order to mortify the flesh and live nearer to God had resorted to a rigid form of asceticism. How much better it would have been had he simply trusted the cleansing Blood for purity of heart and life! There is a danger that many today may seek to find the way of holiness by negative means rather than by positive faith. While self-denial and self-control of bodily appetites and mental powers are very important in spiritual life, they cannot secure for one a pure heart.

Another extreme of how one may be affected by the aesthetic nature of things was illustrated years ago by a very dear and spiritual-minded lady in the southland. She was well past middle life at this time but nonetheless agile and used to walk a considerable distance to church. Quite often she would wear a bright-red dress. If anyone chanced to mention her dress she would reply with lightened countenance, "Praise the Lord, I wear a red dress for the blood of Jesus, which He shed for me!" A strange association indeed but one which apparently brought pleasure to the child of God.

Perhaps it would not be amiss to call attention to the fact here that we should not become harsh judges of what colors people choose to wear, especially women. Whatever best suits the complexion, hair, and other features, and whatever makes the person appear at his best, should certainly not be condemned. Modesty and economy are all the Word has said about the rule for dress; and should we say more? (I Tim. 2:9-10; I Pet. 3:3-4.)

There must be a safeguard set up by all of us against this natural tendency within man toward the love of the beautiful. In itself it is harmless, but if allowed to go to extremes it can become harmful. For example, a housewife can so love beautiful flowers that she neglects her duty to her family in the care of them, or spends more of the income than can be afforded for endless varieties. A man may be so attracted to nature's beauties that he neglects the house of God on Sundays to go into the fields and woodlands. Or one may spend extravagantly for beautiful clothes, thus feeding his natural vanity to the point where pride is gendered in the heart. Likewise one may fill his home with more expensive furnishings than he can afford or than is in keeping with his work or community standing. Some people have gone to extremes to beautify their bodies and in so doing have lost that most lovely of all beauty, the natural beauty which springs from a well-watered soul and a body kept as the temple of the Holy Spirit. Certainly one must never neglect the proper care of his body nor try to cramp its natural appearance by unnatural practices. As the temple of the Holy Spirit it should be kept at all times at its best in cleanliness and proper attire.

One word more may be added respecting the manner of dress. It is wise to dress always in that form of attire which is most becoming to the personality. The young should not strive to appear older, and perhaps it is hardly wise for the older person to try always to appear far more youthful than he is. Let the manner of dress be always as inconspicuous as possible and avoid extremes of the fashions of the times. If one is extreme in his dress, it only serves to attract attention to himself, however modest it may be in form. By this we refer not to proper dress but to those extremes which some would be driven to by Satan in order that the cause of Christ may thereby be reproached. Let no worldling in dress suppose this a license for his attire.

Chapter IX

Differences in
Constitutional Make-up

It seems at first thought that a matter so commonly accepted should have little place in a treatise such as this. But upon further consideration it is apparent from both experience and observation that the failure of many people to understand their own problems is in large measure due to the fact that they do not understand their own constitutional make-up. One's natural disposition can be a source of discouragement to him in his endeavor to live the Spirit-filled life if he does not understand it. Others are greatly aided by this factor without any comprehensive knowledge of its benefits to them.

This may be illustrated by the following example: The writer once knew very well a fine lady who did not profess entire sanctification but in her natural disposition she was so calm and self-possessed as to put to shame some who did. With her it was not inward grace which caused her to be so self-possessed but a constitutional make-up which gave her poise and emotional balance which many others did not possess. There are persons who by nature are sunny-dispositioned and who seldom have a cloud in their sky. It is not always all of grace but sometimes the gift of a well-balanced constitution which makes this true. It is also true that some of these same people at a different period in their lives run into great difficulty because in the changing process of nature their constitutional make-up becomes disordered and they cannot maintain the same calm which they did in former years. Sometimes such persons suffer great mental anguish in fear that they have lost this grace of Christian holiness out of their hearts when in reality it is only the change which nature has thrust upon their bodies. It should be recognized for what it is and the person so affected should refuse to worry about it. But this is often easier advised than done. One must take hold of himself and face the facts squarely, then act accordingly.

On the other hand there are some persons whose constitutional make-up is of a high tension, nervous type. Such persons are generally very sensitive, easily impressed, highly imaginative, and emotionally balanced so delicately that they have difficulty remaining poised. They are easily excited and tend toward quick reaction. With this type of constitution it is easy to see how some people suffer from lack of ability to always meet every situation with that perfect poise which they see in others, and for which they often long. A person of this type may sometimes be subjected to keen accusations from Satan. He will suggest that if there were perfect love in the heart there would be more perfect balance in the disposition. But this is not always true.

Baldwin has well stated this case:

> Holiness people differ temperamentally just as much as they do in other ways. Some are quick, others slow; some are impulsive, others look before they leap; some are open-hearted, while others are more reserved; some are precise, while others are more inclined to be careless; some are very particular about their appearance, while others care very little for such details (as they call them); and so on to the end.[5]

Sometimes people have difficulty getting along with persons of a very different disposition from their own. Younger Christians are apt to think the other person slow, stupid or just careless when he is of that tendency to be more slow and reserved. The person with a fast tempo may be looked upon by the reserved person as impatient, hasty and flighty. Neither may be the case. It is often the difference between the two types of personality which makes the difference rather than any personal weakness. Even mature Christians may misjudge sometimes, as was the case with Mr. Wesley. "Wesley tells of a mistress and maid, who before they were sanctified, were a great trial to each other. When they both obtained this blessing he suggested that doubtless their differences were a thing of the past; but to his surprise, he found that the same incompatibility remained."[6]

One should cultivate greatheartedness and try to understand his fellow Christians. It is often more misunderstanding than evil disposition which causes some persons to question others. The more one cultivates a sympathetic spirit and tries to understand the basic underlying causes for the behavior of another, the more likely he is to see the good and recognize much of what he once thought was evil to be merely human reaction. He who sometimes shouts loudest, "I am not going to compromise with old carnality!" when he sees someone act in a way which he thinks unbecoming to a professor of full salvation, is likely to need the grace of Christian charity to cover some of his own faults.

Sometimes the super-sensitive person whose constitutional make-up is high-strung suffers much inward pain. At times they may sink down in depression even lower than the more reserved or even the extrovert. They often suffer keen temptations made more acute by their highly imaginative minds. Sometimes the high goals which they have set for themselves and seemingly have failed to attain constitute a difficulty for them in this respect also, and they tend to accuse themselves for failure of which in reality they are not guilty. The following incident from the life of John Fletcher may serve to illustrate to what depths of despondency one may go.

It must not be supposed that so holy a man as Fletcher had no temptations. He told Wesley how Satan had often tempted him to put an end to his own life. He was so passionate by nature that he often pled and prayed the whole night to get victory over his temper, and sometimes lay prone upon the floor in an agony of grief as he pled with God for victory; and yet he was famous for his gentleness. In his *Life of Fletcher,* Wesley says: "For twenty years and upwards before his death, no one ever saw him out of temper, or heard him utter a rash expression, on any provocation whatever."[7]

Perhaps it would be well here to give a little further attention to the matter of setting goals beyond one's ability. This may arise from a feeling of inferiority and the desire to achieve something of consequence by which to satisfy the demand to be appreciated. This feeling within itself is not sinful but a natural result of a conclusion which the individual has reached about himself, whether right or wrong. Sometimes one may discover that he is not basically inferior to others if he took the pains to make a few tests. And it is important for everyone to achieve something of worth in life to have a sense of personal value. This may be done best by giving one's self wholly to God and allowing Christ to work in him the spiritual work which will give him eternal value. But he will also be much happier if he can achieve something in the way of Christian service by which to develop a sense of worthwhileness. In attempting to achieve this something persons often resort to setting goals for themselves, either as spiritual heights to be attained or work to be done, which can sometimes become a source of frustration if not fulfilled. Psychologists recognize this as a contributing factor to much mental and emotional unhappiness, whatever be the original cause or motive of the setting of the goals too high the final results are much the same in the individual failing to achieve it, especially if he allows the frustration to proceed to a serious point. Note the following observation:

There are individual differences in the source of frustration, and, more particularly, in the type of reaction to frustration or in the ability to adjust to frustration. The individual who sets goals far beyond his level of achievement seeks certain disappointment. The reaction to the discrepancy between what is and what one wants to be may be very strong and can be understood only when we consider what far-flung goals had been set. The establishment and failure to reach these impossible goals is a neurotic tendency. The feeling of failure and worthlessness, which, to the outside observer, seem completely unjustified and nonunderstandable, are but a phase of neurotic maladjustment.[8]

One must not conclude from this that all goals of achievement are dangerous and therefore should be avoided. Rather, he should endeavor to face himself squarely and accept his limitations, then set his goals somewhere in the neighborhood of what he is reasonably sure can be accomplished. And yet there must be a place for *faith* in everyone's program of life goals. It is certain that many men have achieved far beyond that they or anyone else in their youth believed them to be capable of doing. This they did by faith in God and in themselves. If one is to accept the challenge of only what he can see he will greatly circumscribe himself and come far short of his full best in life. The better thing for one to do, then, in the face of both circumstances, is to set his sights to achieve the most possible good both personally in soul and service-wise for Christ that he can, and keep always the attitude that it is better to die with a goal only partially achieved than to have had one unworthy of himself and to have met it fully. If this attitude be sustained to old age there will be no danger of frustration from unfulfilled goals.

It might be well for parents who are very conscientious about rearing their children properly to keep this in mind. Many a mother especially has suffered untold mental anguish because her children did not achieve in life the goals which she had set for them. If parents have done their reasonable best and have constantly prayed with and for their children, lived consistently before them and taught them properly they can rest their case in God's hands and refuse to worry about it. This again is much easier advised than done. But one must remember that parents cannot set the final goals toward which their children will steer. They can only assist them in making them the most worthy types of goals, and sometimes they fail here through no fault of their own.

Whatever one's particular type of constitutional make-up may be, his best step for happiness is to become as well acquainted with himself as possible. When one knows his weaknesses and his strength, his temperamental gait and his ability to speed or slow it up; when he has his hands quite safely upon the emotional controls of his mind and body, he is in shape for fair sailing on life's sea. But let him beware always for no ship is safe in some types of storm.

It should perhaps be further pointed out that one's constitutional make-up is subject to change with the advancing years of life. This was pointed out above briefly but may we add that many persons have considerable difficulty making the voyage of life successfully because they do not make the proper adjustments to each successive period in life. As Allport has well pointed out, "A single life history, when fully studied, shows an orderly and necessary process of growth, each stage being the necessary result of what has gone before." This "includes differentiation, integration, maturation, and learning as different aspects of growth."[9]

When one tries to cling too long or too strongly to any one period of life he does so at his ultimate peril. Most young people long to get out of the teens and get on with life. Most people move progressively along with life's program until about mid-life or a bit older. At this period some develop recessive tendencies and show an unwillingness to go on to older years. The inconveniences of age are either dreaded or feared and the person tries to make himself believe he is "as good as ever!" He speaks of feeling "as well as I did at twenty-five," and uses similar devices to avoid accepting his age. All this may look innocent to undiscerning persons and even seem so to those engaging in it but if the person so attempting to escape his age remains serious in this attempt he will thwart nature's purpose and pave the way for trouble in his emotional and mental life.

Every age or period has its compensations and he who tries to live through one period in the memory of another will lose none of them and become a person belonging realistically to neither. What mid-life lacks in agility it should make up for in wisdom and the solid comfort of having well loved its youth. "The head should save the heel" at this period in life. Rather than looking back longingly for the good old days of youth one should make these the good old days to which in further age he can look back with the satisfaction of having given himself to them at his best. Changes in constitutional reactions and bodily conditions should be accepted for what they are—signs of advancing age—and nothing to be worried about. Further discussion of emotional reactions and how to handle them will be discussed in a later chapter.

Chapter X

Differences in Receptivity of Light

There are varying degrees in the differences of receptivity of light in different individuals and in the same individual at different times there may also be a quicker and a slower pace in receiving light. For example, two persons of near equal opportunities in education and spiritual attainments may listen to the same minister and hear the same truth for the first time about a certain thing of Christian practice, say tithing. One will almost immediately proclaim that he sees this to be his duty. After considerable time the other person finally announces that he has become convinced from an article he read or someone's testimony that he should tithe his income. For him the minister's message brought no new light.

Lincicome says:

> Sanctified people differ in their moral and spiritual perceptions. This is due to two things, namely, inheritance and enlightenment. It is due many times to inheritance. Some of us are very slow to comprehend. We cannot see the moral quality of an action as quickly as others. . . . We are slow to comprehend the meaning of many Scriptural utterances, but if given time we will see it. Then this difference in moral and spiritual perception is due to enlightenment. Some have more light than others for the simple reason that light comes by degrees. What do we mean by light? . . . A Bible definition of light reads, "Whatsoever doth make manifest is light."[10]

Light does not come to one except by the revelation of the Holy Spirit to the consciousness. This may be done in many ways, as in the preaching of the Word, studying the Word, by the printed page, the testimony of another and sometimes from acts of providence or in meditation. But whatever instrument is employed the Holy Spirit is still the Agent who "manifests" this light to the soul.

The reception of light is progressive from the first rays of conviction for sin to the last manifestation of God's will to the mature saint before his being taken to glory. Generally, the rate of progress is much more rapid in the early stages of the Christian experience. This is normal. It is at this time that much light concerning one's spiritual welfare and means of progress is needed. The learning process is always more rapid earlier in life. If an adult could learn as much proportionately each year after twenty-one that he did the first ten years of his life he would become an intellectual giant, mastering far beyond anything we now can comprehend. New light keeps pace with new spiritual progress in the soul and new responsibility likewise follows close upon the heels of new light.

One should never condemn himself as stupid or slow of heart because he has not seen certain light before. When it dawns it seems anyone should have seen a thing so simple as this but it is not always so. There may be reasons unknown to us for which it was withheld. It is enough to rejoice in it now and go on. Christ is our light and by Him we march on our way heavenward.

One must continually guard against Satan taking occasion to mislead one by "false light." He may come as "an angel of light" and so impress one as to make him feel he will sin if he does not obey this or that impression. Wesley warned:

> Do not easily ascribe things to God. Do not easily suppose dreams, voices, impressions, visions, or revelations to be from God. They may be from Him; they may be from

nature; they may be from the devil. Therefore "believe not every spirit, but try the spirits whether they be of God." Try all things by the written word, and let all bow down before it. You are in danger of enthusiasm (fanaticism) if you depart ever so little from Scripture.[11]

Differences in
Ability to Perform

Sometimes Spirit-filled persons are sorely tried by Satan because they cannot perform various services like others. In the earlier days of one's Spirit-filled experience Satan sometimes suggests that if he were truly filled with the Spirit as he claims to be he would be able to perform this or that service with "power" and ease. The emphasis upon "power" made by some Christian leaders who emphasize this element of the Spirit's baptism even to the neglect of purity of heart which it produces tends to heighten this sense of inadequacy in persons whose talents for public service are limited or undeveloped. Wiseman has well said:

> Biblical perfection takes into account the measure of man's capacity and ability. People greatly differ in this regard, and as a consequence differ in the degree of love and service, but in every case it is loving God with all one's powers. It should be remembered that all Divine love is perfect. The perfection of love has reference to quantity rather than quality. The clean heart has more room for God and the fulness of His love than has an unsanctified heart.[12]

One may have a perfect heart filled with perfect love to God and yet render an imperfect service to God. This may be illustrated as follows. Two brooms are standing in the closet, one with a red handle, the other being green. The mother tells her little four-year-old girl to bring the broom. The child immediately obeys, bringing the one with the red handle to which she was naturally attracted first, not noticing that it had a broken handle. Here is a perfect obedience but an imperfect service. The brooms must be exchanged but could that mother scold her child justly? Certainly not. Likewise we may often render to God and our fellowmen an imperfect service while with our heart we are in perfect accord with the divine will so far as we understand it. Our heads are often at fault when our hearts are sure.

One should never become discouraged because he cannot witness as well as another so far as fluent speech is concerned. The witness of a person whose words are slow and even stammering is as important as that of the gifted speaker. There are times, indeed, when it will be more convincing. To some people the gifted conversationalist is not a convincing person at all but the one who measures his words and speaks with a sense of conviction is far more powerful in moving them. It is the sincerity of what one says more than the manner in which he says it that has the most lasting effect.

On the other hand one can often improve his talents if he will apply himself. If God has laid it upon one's heart to do a certain type of Christian work He is also prepared to aid that person in becoming able to perform the task. After pointing out that there are differences in the capacities of sanctified people Lincicome says:

> There are some things that we can do to enlarge our capacity, and we ought to do it, for it not only increases our happiness here, but will increase it forever more. One of those things that will enlarge our capacities is the baptism of the Holy Spirit. There is nothing that we can do that will release the energies of our souls, that will bring out and develop latent qualities of our hearts, like the baptism with the Holy Spirit.[18]

Even after the baptism with the Holy Spirit has been experienced there will still be a difference in the capacity of believers to perform in service. But growth in grace and knowledge will be much faster for those who have had this experience, and the Spirit will "help our infirmities" in overcoming the shyness, natural fears or other things which would hinder us.

Section Three

Difficulties of the Spirit-filled Life

And every man that striveth for the mastery is temperate in all things. Now they do it to obtain a corruptible crown; but we an incorruptible. I therefore so run, not as uncertainly; so fight I, not as one that beateth the air: but I keep under my body, and bring it into subjection: lest that by any means, when I have preached to others, I myself should be a castaway (I Cor. 9:25-27).

And he said unto me, My grace is sufficient for thee: for my strength is made perfect in weakness. Most gladly therefore will I rather glory in my infirmities, that the power of Christ may rest upon me. Therefore I take pleasure in infirmities, in reproaches, in necessities, in persecutions, in distresses for Christ's sake: for when I am weak, then am I strong (II Cor. 12:9-10).

CHAPTER XII

Reconciling
the Human and Divine Life

Life is a series of problems broken in spots with what we are pleased to call "happiness." Without these problems, life would cease to be human life as we know it. But this in no sense takes the joy out of living nor makes life too difficult.

That there are difficulties in Spirit-filled living no experienced person of this life will deny, but these problems can be successfully met and solved by those who diligently try. Our purpose here is to offer suggestions which may be found helpful in reconciling these difficulties with the Spirit-filled life. All difficulties arising can either be solved by removing the difficulty if this is possible or finding how to cope with it if it be a circumstance beyond one's control. St. Paul did not get deliverance from his "thorn in the flesh," but he did find grace in Christ to endure it "gladly" for Christ's sake.

Not all the difficulties which may arise in the sanctified life can here be dealt with, but an attempt is made to cover the most outstanding ones which have come to our attention over the years.

St. Paul said of this blessed Spirit-filled life, "But we have this treasure in earthen vessels, that the excellency of the power may be of God, and not of us" (II Cor. 4:7). It is reported that Rev. Joseph H. Smith once quoted this, "We have this treasure in earthen vessels," then added in his quaint way, "and some of the vessels are a little cracked."

No amount of grace which one may receive in life will ever take him beyond the realm of the human element. Despite the fact that the heart is cleansed from sin, the human factors still remain, as has been well stated:

> Errors of judgment, infirmities of body, fears occasioned by surprise, unpleasant dreams, wandering thoughts in prayer, times when there is no joy, a sense of inefficiency in Christian labor, and strong temptations, are by no means inconsistent with perfect love. Yet errors need the atonement.[1]

It is difficult to conceive how the very eternal God, in the person of the Holy Spirit, can so dispose himself as to come into the narrow confines of human personality and there dwell. The Apostle Paul is not to be taken mystically when he says, "Know ye not that your body is the temple of the Holy Ghost which is in you, which ye have of God, and ye are not your own?" (I Cor. 6:19) The Spirit of God does in very reality abide in the heart of those who have been filled with His holy presence.

How it is that He can indwell each and every believer's heart individually and personally is a mystery which none can explain. He adds nothing to the human spirit as such but pure love and detracts nothing from it but sin. He fills one's innermost being without overflowing his essential personality. He controls one's emotions or aids him in so doing without dictating his actions and governs his will without directing it. How this inner fullness abides without disturbing personality cannot be explained any more than one can explain how two persons in deep and fervent love become a part of each other so that "they twain shall be one flesh" (Matt. 19:5). One may illustrate crudely by referring to an ordinary can of motor oil into which another small can of far more highly refined oil can be poured, with the motor oil container already full, yet without overflowing it. The less refined oil will absorb the more refined among the molecules which do not lie so closely together as those of the more refined oil. This materialization of the Spirit in no way occurs in His filling our hearts, any more than two people in the depths of married love cease to be two persons and merge into one. But the illustration serves only to dimly shadow how He fills us without overflowing us. Or again, one may sit in an audience of ten thousand and see and hear the President of the United States deliver an address. He will receive the full benefit of the President's personality and speech to the uttermost of his capacity to understand and appreciate him just as fully as if there were no other listeners there, yet the rest of the audience will receive equal to their capacity. The one in no way detracts from the masses, and the masses in no way detract from the one.

This brings us to the consideration of keeping the proper balance of relationship between the human element and the divine element in the life. The Spirit-filled life is not all of God nor all of human endeavor but a co-operative venture. On the human side there must be constant devotion and a keeping of the powers of mind and body under the Spirit's control. From the Spirit's side there flows always the grace sufficient for this task. One cannot so fully be absorbed in God that he loses his identity with the world. Such mystics as Fenelon and Madam Guyon apparently tried this, but while these rare spirits rose to great spiritual heights they nevertheless continued to have their earth-bound existence,[2] and sometimes bitter disillusionments that they could not be fully freed from the trials of the flesh. Nor should one so totally depend upon the Spirit to supply grace that he neglects the proper means of grace. It will require the best there is in every man to live the Spirit-filled life at its best. But God's Spirit will also aid the believer in his part of work and service, as one has observed:

> The Spirit not only prepares believers for the service of God by bestowing on them all His spiritual gifts, but also accompanies them step by step in the achievement of

their alloted task . . . (Acts 13:4, 8-9; 16:6, 7) . . . It was thus the early Christians made their conquest of the Roman Empire and that their efforts bore such fruit in abundance.[3]

The Spirit-filled life is a conquest for the best in life for the individual and the highest service to his fellow men in co-operation with the indwelling Holy Spirit.

CHAPTER XIII

Difficulties Arising from Faults

One may be "blameless and harmless," a son of God, and yet at the same time have certain faults which still cling to him. There is no experience in grace which will entirely free one from some form of faults, although the indwelling Holy Spirit will keep the believer in the attitude to correct his faults where possible and rectify any mistakes. One difficulty with some faults is that in the attempt to cure one a person may fall into another. For instance, let one be told that he talks too much for his own good and that of others, and sometimes he will fall into the other extreme of trying to say as little as possible, only to be misunderstood again as being peeved about something. To properly correct a fault is no small task in many instances.

It is fortunate that we do not all have the same faults and yet that there are enough similarities to keep each one humble as he thinks of his own.

Faults or mistakes are not properly sins. Taylor asks, "By the term 'sin' do we include every mistake in judgment, unknown offense, or other manifestation of human frailty and limitation? Obviously not . . . let us remember, first, that God's quarrel is not with our humanity, but with our disposition to set our will against His." It was Taylor's opinion that God would rather live with a "stupid, illiterate peasant who loved Him with a complete love" than with a perfect Adam who made no errors except to choose his own will against that of God's. He could correct and polish the poor peasant, but the perfect Adam would still be disobedient at heart.[4] God desires our loving obedience, and when this is rendered fully it is acceptable even if sometimes done in an imperfect manner.

Some have difficulty in distinguishing between sins and mistakes, but let it be clear that "a mistake is not a sin; neither is a sin a mistake. A mistake comes from the head, while a sin proceeds from an evil principle in the heart. There are a wicked choice and a bad motive back of a sin, but neither of these is back of a mistake."[5] Mistakes may be responsible for serious results and yet be innocent. The switchman may mistake a signal and allow the train to proceed through an open switch, plunging the crew and passengers into a fearful wreck, and yet be innocent of any guilt for his mistake. A mistaken idea about something may lead to a mistake in application to everyday life, but unless the person involved has discovered his mistake in time to become responsible for the act growing out of it, he can hardly be held culpable. Wesley said:

> A man may be filled with pure love, and still be liable to mistake. Indeed, I do not expect to be freed from actual mistake till this mortal puts on immortality. I believe this to be a natural consequence of the soul's dwelling in the flesh and blood. . . . A mistake in opinion may occasion a mistake in practice. Every such mistake is a transgression of the perfect law. Therefore, every such mistake, were it not for the blood of atonement, would expose to eternal damnation. It follows that the most perfect have continual need of the merits of Christ, even for their actual transgressions, and may say for themselves, as well as for their brethren, "Forgive us our trespasses."[6]

In concluding this portion with respect to faults and imperfections let it be noted that hardly can anyone who is wholly aware of his own weaknesses speak lightly of those of another. Everyone should practice daily the spirit and work of that apostolic injunction, "Brethren, if a man be overtaken in a fault, ye which are spiritual, restore such an one in the spirit of meekness; considering thyself, lest thou also be tempted" (Gal. 6:1). While this passage doubtless refers to a more serious incident than a mere "mistake" or ordinary fault, yet it sets the pace for the spiritual attitude of all toward anyone who may be in error, great or small.

With respect to our human limitations and weaknesses, viewed in the light of Christ's infirmities, it may be well to give here the saintly Fletcher's remarks about the Saviour:

> Was not our Lord Himself imperfect? Did His bodily strength never fail in agonizing prayer? or in intense labor? Did His animal spirits ever move with the same sprightliness? Do we not read of His sleeping in the ship when His disciples wrestled with the tempestuous sea? Did He not fulfil the precept, "Be ye angry, and sin not", Had He not the troublesome sensation of grief at Lazarus' grave, of hunger in the wilderness, of weariness at Jacob's well, and of thirst upon the cross? If He was "made in the likeness of sinful flesh," and "tempted in all things as we are," is it not highly probable that He was not an utter stranger to the natural appetites and uneasy sensations which are incident to flesh and blood? Is it a sin to feel them? Is it not rather a virtue totally to deny them, or not to satisfy them out of the line of duty, or not to indulge them in an excessive manner on that line?[7]

Certainly, the "disciple is not above his master . . . It is enough for the disciple that he be as his master" (Matt. 10:24-25).

CHAPTER XIV

Controlling Our Bodies

The proper control of the body is one of the most important things in the Spirit-filled believer's life. Sanctification does not destroy any normal bodily appetite. It affects the body only as it is affected through the Spirit. St. Paul affirms this when he says, "Every sin that a man doeth is without the body" (I Cor. 6:18). The body is but the instrument of the spirit of man. It is neither good nor bad except as it is employed by the spirit. Its appetites are normal so long as they are kept in proper control, and only the spirit of man stands condemned when they are allowed to go out of proper bounds. But the body as a living organism makes constant demands for the satisfaction of its appetites. Nor can one well separate the soulish demands from those of the body. The desire of social fellowship, grasp for possession, and outward reach for varying forms of satisfaction must also be guarded.

St. Paul found it necessary even after his sanctification to hold all his powers in check. "But I keep under my body, and bring it into subjection: lest that by any means, when I have preached to others, I myself should be a castaway" (I Cor. 9:27). The Greek here rendered, "I keep under my body," is rather peculiar. It refers to that part of the face below the eye; hence, to "strike one beneath the eye; to beat black and blue." It means rigid discipline of the body, keeping it under control.[8] Concerning the mental powers the same apostle announced his policy in no uncertain terms when he said, "Casting down imaginations [reasonings], and every high thing that exalteth itself against the knowledge of God, and bringing into captivity every thought to the obedience of Christ" (II Cor. 10:5). Here then is Paul's picture of how the whole man is controlled and kept constantly in submission to Christ.

The Holy Spirit does not automatically control our lives but rather gives us grace to control ourselves and power to hold in check those native tendencies and appetites which, though not sinful in themselves, would become so if allowed to be satisfied in illegitimate ways. There is of course a certain area in which the Holy Spirit seems to control certain of our emotions almost automatically. Take for example the emotion of fear as it relates to God. Carnal fear is removed by sanctifying grace, so that at the thought of God there arises in the soul automatically the trusting attitude instead of the former terror. Although it must be said that the holiest of men still maintain a sense of the fear of God, it is not slavish fear.

Or the emotion of hate may be used to illustrate. When someone did harm to us or used us meanly in past times, hate would bounce to the surface before we could control our inner emotions. But now since perfect love reigns there is no sense or feeling of hate but automatically that of good will. However one cannot keep the suggestions of Satan at the moment of attack from entering his mind as to how to repay the offender, but he has no inward response of his will to accommodate these suggestions with action. He may feel the sense of self-defense or bodily protection arise if the offense is of such a nature as to warrant such action.

Some persons not distinguishing between this sense which is perfectly natural and the other sense of spitefulness toward the offender have been greatly troubled at times. But the natural sense passes away with the ceasing of its necessity whereas the carnal sense of spiteful intention remains and rankles in the soul.

To control the body properly one must be on the alert and be watchful against any satanic intrusions. But this should not amount to a slavish guarding of the body. When the soul is kept in communion with God, and the Holy Spirit abides within one's heart, God will always see to it that one is properly warned when he is in any danger. Then, too, when one establishes certain basic behavior patterns for his body and mind, the very constitutional make-up of mind and body come to his aid in that they tend to follow these established patterns. The longer one lives the Spirit-filled life, the more fully he yields himself to God, the more ready will be his response to the gentle tugs of the Spirit upon the reins of his mind when he is warned thereby of impending danger.

And yet it must be admitted that at no time in life, even to old age, will life become so systematized that it will "run itself." And sometimes after many years of righteous living one is almost astounded to find that some bodily appetite which he thought well governed comes to the surface and demands satisfaction with an amazing force. He must then arise to the occasion and put it in its place. This is no sign of reigning sin within the heart nor necessarily of a lapse spiritually. It may be the changing condition of the body or the slant with which the suggestion struck the mind at the moment of attack which accounts for it. And do not be surprised if it recurs several times before it is subdued. For if it provides a shock emotionally when it occurs, a channel has been opened for its recurrence, which is psychologically as natural as for water to follow a course already established. And if Satan sees that this is true, he may be expected to attack again and again in an attempt to break through at what he sees as a "weak spot." To "worry over it" will not help. Rather, it may serve to help strengthen the appeal and weaken the resistance. Bring it quickly to the Lord's attention and commit it afresh to Him. The Holy Spirit may be depended upon in such an hour to come to the defense of one being so tried.

The matter of evil thoughts often bothers Spirit-filled persons until they learn more about their relationship to such a life. One cannot help thoughts of evil from being presented to the mind, for otherwise there could be no temptation. Christ in the wilderness was presented by Satan with thoughts of evil. But there is a difference between *thoughts of evil* as suggestions to the mind, arising either from Satan's attack or from natural circumstances by which they are often presented, and *evil thoughts* as arising from the inward heart. The former are promptly rejected. The latter is something one secretly cherishes and holds within himself until the whole course of his imagination or passions is set on fire by them. Hadfield puts it well when, after discussing the opinion that to allow the thought to present itself, then reject it, is wiser than the attempt to ignore entirely the very fact of its presence, he says:

> The injunction of Christ about not "looking on a woman to lust after her" is not hostile to this principle. Incidentally, the injunction particularly referred to the *married woman* (*gunaika*), and was therefore made in the interest of the monogamous principle. But more important, the context shows that it was concerned with *intention* to lust, which is very different from the impulse or deisre.[*]

The natural appetites may be appealed to by various forms of presentation over which the person has no control. The basic biological urges may even be affected by such presentations at times, to the utter dismay of those who are thus affected. But this does not constitute sin nor carnal desire in any sense so long as there is no act of the will to accept the suggestions presented. The fine, hairsplitting accusations of Satan or of the person to himself, Did I or did I not for a split second accept the suggestions? can almost always be settled by examining the motive or the will. Was my will set to obey God? Did I secretly cherish this and accept it? The Spirit-filled person immediately realizes that his whole heart cries out, Never! However keen the presentation or sense of appeal may have been, one is assured of no sinful response so long as the will did not co-operate. If there is still any question, cast the whole matter upon the Lord, for we are told that "if in any thing we be otherwise minded, God shall reveal even this unto you" (Phil. 3:15). If there is no lasting sense of condemnation, it is sure that no evil has clung to the soul.

Sometimes the appeal of the natural appetites is illustrated in this manner. One who especially likes apples may go down the street past an open market where large, luscious red apples are on display. Immediately the saliva arises in one's mouth without his being able to control it. The biological urges know no moral laws; they respond to sight or smell, irrespective of any moral issues that may be thereafter involved. But the person has no money with him to purchase the fruit and legitimately satisfy the appetite. But he does have the will power not to take it from the stand without paying for it. Now as he turns away after having been strongly appealed to by his appetite, did he "covet" because the natural response arose uncontrollably? No! Covetousness would have entered had he willfully tried to scheme some way in his mind to secure this fruit without paying for it by sneaking it from the stand. This illustration may serve to cover a whole field of natural desires and appetites and how one is to control them or look upon their responses when they have been affected by strong appeals.

Attention should be given also to how far one may go in the satisfying of legitimate desires in proper ways. Much in this field must depend upon the individual concerned. One man may eat a large, hearty meal with complete freedom while another must be contented to partake sparingly because of his condition. While it most certainly is wrong to constantly overeat to the detriment of the body, it is just as certainly not sinful to overeat sometimes more or less by accident. One often does not feel he has overeaten until well afterward. This is not gluttony but poor judgment.

There is also the matter of securing possessions, which, while not a bodily matter, may affect the body. When a man pushes himself beyond his capacity and breaks his health for the sake of securing possessions beyond his necessary needs, he does wrong.

> The power of money to wean the affections away from God can be seen among the poor as well as among the rich. The worldly cares that arise in the quest cause trouble for all alike, and worldly cares are just as destructive of the soul as worldly pleasures. They are just as "vain and shameful, and as sensual gratifications when they . . . divide or possess the heart.[10]

Many a man has shortened his days of usefulness by driving his body past its ability in order to secure even more possessions. In so doing most men have robbed their souls of the best in life. Often their families have suffered because of it, and the cause of Christ has suffered. Even if they have contributed well, their personal life of piety has been seriously affected and their influence impaired.

We turn now to the more delicate matter of difficulties which sometimes arise respecting proper sex relations between married couples. There are many angles to this problem and a set rule cannot always be arrived at because conditions of health, circumstances, the other partner's needs, and various other things enter into this complicated problem. But there are a few basic principles that should not be overlooked.

First, it is clear that proper sexual relations are normal for married couples and are not to be condemned, as some have taught. The notion that sexual relations are to be avoided except for purposes of procreation is entirely foreign to the teachings of the New Testament upon this subject. In St. Paul's instructions to married couples in I Cor. 7:1-6 he specifically admonishes in verse 5, "Defraud ye not one the other, except it be with consent for a time, that ye may give yourselves to fasting and prayer; and come together again, that Satan tempt you not for your incontinency." No language can be plainer than this. The fact that he spoke it not "by commandment" but "by permission" does not change the fact that it was evidently sanctioned by the Lord. Otherwise, it would have hardly been allowed to become a part of his instruction. St. Peter also admonished, "Likewise, ye husbands, dwell with them according to knowledge, giving honour to the wife, as unto the weaker vessel, and as being heirs together of the grace of life; that your prayers be not hindered" (I Pet. 3:7). This injunction seems to connect proper sexual relationships and marital relations in general with spiritual life, emphasizing the fact that failure here could spell "hindered" prayers for the persons concerned.

On I Cor. 7:5, Clarke observes:

> It is most evident that the separations *permitted* by the apostle, for he *enjoins* none, are only for a *season,* on extraordinary occasions; and that the persons *may come together again,* lest Satan, taking advantage of their matrimonial abstinence, might tempt either to illicit commerce.[11]

Sometimes the attempt of one partner to be more self-denying in matters of sexual relations than is normally proper has brought considerable difficulty and even sorrow into an otherwise happy marriage. Occasionally the Christian partner seems to lose interest in this part of married life because the other is unsympathetic with his spiritual life. Naturally, any emotional jar can bring discord into this most delicate of all human relations. Such discords are to be expected even in the lives of the most spiritual at times. But the Christian companion must find some basis of emotional response if the happiness of the home is to be saved. Often the unchristian companion is won by the tender affectionate response of the spouse, whereas he may be driven completely away by the careless companion who puts his own wishes first. Does not this perfect love for God and man give the Christian companion the desire to be the best possible partner rather than draw him away from his spouse? Each person in such circumstances must prayerfully discover the best way to live successfully with his unsaved companion and yet retain his proper spiritual balance. And this God will help him to do. But it can seldom, if ever, be done by denying the other partner his rightful place in proper sexual relationships.

A couple who are fully adjusted spiritually may still have difficulties which will need to be adjusted from time to time. To offer complete counsel is beyond the scope of this work, but it should here be pointed out that the mutual satisfying of each partner so that a harmony of marital relations is maintained is a goal well worthy of the best attempts of every couple. Too rigid a program of self-denial may produce unhappy effects in both the emotional and the mental realms. On the other hand, constant and excessive indulgence contributes to degeneracy of emotional, mental, and spiritual powers. A common-sense approach to this as to all other problems is always best. Where difficulties arise which the couple cannot solve themselves successfully, they should not hesitate to seek the advice of a physician. Sometimes the counsel of a minister is also of inestimable value, especially where he is prepared to give such counsel. And many times the advice of the pastor who has had no special training can be most helpful. Often couples by endeavoring to "keep their troubles to themselves" have suffered much unnecessarily which competent counsel could have saved.

How far a person may go in the enjoyment of any innocent pleasure or pastime, or in the exercise of any legitimate recreation of body or mind, must be governed by several things. The amount of time one has for such things which does not infringe upon other duties or obligations, the need for such recreation, the money to spare without taking from others what is due them, and the proper place where such things may be done with credit to the person as a Spirit-filled believer—these all enter into it. One must always keep close enough to the Master to hear the whispering of the Spirit when He would check him if he is going beyond what is good for him. Each person must decide for himself under the leadership of the Spirit what is best for him and how far he may go with it. Sometimes even in common conversation when one has said enough he will feel the check of the Spirit. It pays to obey when this is the case. There may be unknown reasons which we cannot know for which we are checked. Above all else, do not attempt to set the standard by what others do or do not do. One can get into difficulty by this. St. Paul warned that "they measuring themselves . . . are not wise." God's Word and His Spirit's leadings are to be the Christian's standard of conduct at all times.

CHAPTER XV

Understanding Our Infirmities

So long as we are in the body there will always be the problem of our infirmities. With some this poses a greater difficulty than with others because of the extent to which one is affected by them. But all human beings have some form of infirmities. These are not sins but they are weaknesses of the human personality which may be played upon by the devil both as a means to torment the godly person and as an avenue by which sin may enter one's life. That they are not sinful propensities is evident from St. Paul's reference to his own infirmities. "Most gladly therefore will I rather glory in my infirmities, that the power of Christ may rest upon me" (II Cor. 12:9). He even says, "Therefore I take pleasure in infirmities . . . for Christ's sake" (v. 10). It must be remembered that this was said in connection with his "thorn in the flesh" and refers to his glorying in the power of the sufficiency of grace for infirmities to be borne rather than in the infirmity as such. It is for "Christ's sake" that he takes pleasure in such difficulties as arise from infirmities.

Anyone who is afflicted or distressed to the point where special grace is needed to bear it will thereby find that, if taken in the proper attitude, affliction is the means of a ministry of grace sometimes not found outside the domain of suffering. On the other hand, however, Satan often attacks one through his infirmities. At any point where grace may be magnified in one's life, it is only reasonable to expect that Satan will attempt to gain an advantage, that he may thereby militate against God and His work in the human life. For this cause many Spirit-filled believers have difficulties with their infirmities. If the issues which tend to confuse and trouble such persons can be cleared up a bit, it will be well worth the attempt.

The nervous system is the most delicate mechanism known to man. It is at once his best friend and often his most difficult problem. An upset nervous system can make one feel that everything is wrong with him when no organic trouble can be discovered otherwise.

One of the most outstanding tests through which one may pass and yet remain functionally intact is that of a disordered nervous condition. By this is not meant a mental break nor a complete so-called "nervous breakdown," but the milder forms of nervousness due to bodily weakness or nervous exhaustion. In this state the nerves may be so affected as to cause peculiar sensations and strange feelings to come over one, or jumpy, restless, and unwholesome responses to ordinary stimuli. Sometimes in such a state the mere rattling of paper or shuffling of the feet by someone can bring excitement almost unbearable to the one so affected. One may jump or even scream at a very slight excitement and have several of the sensations which normally accompany anger. This is not the slightest sign of any unholy disturbance in the heart but merely the responses of the body under such nervous tension. As one has well said:

> An overtaxed nervous system will cause moods, actions and emotions that resemble carnal impatience, but which do not come from carnality. "An abnormal, diseased condition of the nervous system is no more carnality than measles is smallpox." The nerves affect the mind, and the mind affects the conduct; so we must be more charitable and sympathetic regarding the conduct of a person whose nerves are overtaxed, for they are sure to speak at times with such a tone of voice as would resemble the voice of carnality.[12]

Baldwin has gone to some extent in pointing out the difference between wrought-up nerves and manifestations of carnality.[13] Rasping, disagreeable sensations which chase each other up and down the spine are no more a sign of an impure heart than is the toothache.

In times when the nerves are wrought up, one may feel sinking sensations as if death itself were drawing nigh. Often the mind will become clouded and the spirit droop with depressing feelings. Not a few persons at such times have experienced severe suggestions to the mind that perhaps something is wrong with them spiritually, and should they die, all would not be well. This does not necessarily arise from carnal fear but from the mood in which the person is at that moment. One should then look to God in faith and rest upon Him supremely, refusing to give place to such suggestions for even a moment. At such times it will be necessary to "walk by faith, not by sight." There may appear to be no inward witness to the work of grace in the soul, and Satan may then come to buffet and accuse. But if one holds on to faith and trusts God, resigning all into His hands, he will always come through to sunshine again. When one feels that he is at the bottom, there is this consolation: *One who is on the bottom cannot fall!* Rest upon the mercy of God and in the shed blood of Christ; trust not to human strength nor understanding, no not for an hour, but in the "living God," who delivered us from so great a death, and doth deliver" us even now through Christ.

In his endeavor to trap and ruin mankind, Satan has ever made his greatest attempt through the *mind.* Ever since the fall of man, his mind has been subject to many infirmities. It is little wonder that Satan, having accomplished his master stroke in Eden by gaining the attention and co-operation of the minds of Adam and Eve, should continue to fight man today through this avenue. When he approached the Lord Jesus in the wilderness temptation, it was through the avenue of His mind. It is still his supreme battlefield with the saints today. St. Paul recognized this in his reference quoted above where he speaks of bringing "into captivity every thought" to Jesus Christ. As a safeguard against the encroachment of the enemy in this area, Paul exhorted the Philippian Christians to "let this mind be in you, which was also in Christ Jesus" (Phil. 2:5). Again we are warned, "For consider him that endured such contradiction of sinners against himself, lest ye be wearied and faint in your minds" (Heb. 12:3). St. Peter exhorts, "Wherefore gird up the loins of your mind, be sober" (I Pet. 1:13). Paul reminded Timothy that "God hath not given us the spirit of fear; but of power, and of love, and of a sound mind" (II Tim. 1:7).

The Scriptures nowhere require perfection of mind in order to please God. A "perfect heart" is required and "perfect love" is mentioned as the acme of Christian experience, but perfect knowledge is nowhere required.

Because of the imperfection of the mind there may be many mistakes of mind and of judgment. Sometimes imperfect actions proceed from imperfect judgment, and often the true saint of God is grieved when he sees in the light of more complete knowledge the error of his action. He will be quick to acknowledge his fault and correct his error but this does not remove the fact that it was an error. Perhaps none would claim never to break the "perfect law" of God at some minor point, but there is an unnumerable cloud of witnesses who will readily testify that they do not do so by purpose or intention but only through ignorance or by accident.

Finney well clarifies the difference between perfect knowledge and perfection as required by Christ. Commenting on Matt. 5:48, he says, "The perfection required in the text is not perfection of knowledge, even according to our limited faculties."[14] As we have seen, Wesley did not expect to become exempt from mistakes until death. Doubtless the lack of perfect knowledge is largely to blame for most mistakes in judgment and not a few in other areas. And since God has withheld from man the perfection of knowledge, how could He justly require of him that perfection which alone could come from perfect knowledge? Even the great love chapter (I Corinthians 13) recognizes that there may be perfect love without perfect knowledge.

Many of God's chosen saints have been troubled by *wandering thoughts*. This inability to keep the mind fixed upon a given object, course of thought, or meditation is of itself no more evidence of impurity of heart than is indigestion. It is simply the result of our fallen condition and nothing more. This may happen in respect to temptation. At times when the mind is weary, it will wander aimlessly from one subject to another and one finds it difficult to keep out momentary flights of imagination. At such times it may be that Satan takes advantage to flash upon the screen of the mind evil suggestions and unwholesome thoughts. Elsewhere we have observed:

> In a moment of high tension or pressure, some trifling evil impression comes, or under temptation a very evil thought, perhaps relative to God or His works, flashes across the mind; or perchance while reading the Word some demonical influence showers a tirade of blasphemous and ridiculous ideas upon the screen of the imagination before one scarcely realizes what is happening. A shudder of horror runs over one at such grievous turns of mind. Immediately, here comes the arch-deceiver with sickle in hand to mow him down.[15]

Often one is tempted in the earlier days of his Spirit-filled experience, or when ill health causes these conditions to beset him, to wonder if his heart is truly pure.

How could such imaginations come about if it were? It must be remembered that the mind is subject to every form of impression and from all sources. This is due to the fact that we live in an evil world where the sights and sounds of evil cannot be avoided and that such make an impression upon the mind even when one is not aware of it. It may even be possible that language once heard as a child or scenes of early childhood may lie dormant in the subconscious mind for many years; then at a moment when one has no memory of any such experiences in the past, they come flooding into the imagination as fresh from yesterday but without the accompanying circumstances of the childhood experience. Thus one cannot reconstruct the past and account for the present shower of evil suggestions. But if there is any question as to whether perfect love or sanctification would not have removed all such even from the subconscious memory, we reply, No more than the flood of healthy blood into a section of scar tissue left by a bad accident in the past will remove the scar. Just as the scar tissue may provide a weak spot where another bruise could take place more easily, so the evil thought pattern may provide a means of attack for Satan at a more vulnerable point, but in neither case does the past experience necessarily weaken the resistance of the individual to possible attack.

On this point Wesley observed:

How many wanderings of thought may arise from those various associations of our ideas, which are made entirely without our knowledge, and independently of our choice? How these connections are formed we cannot tell: but they are formed in a thousand different manners. Nor is it in the power of the wisest or holiest of men to break those associations, or to prevent what is the necessary consequence of them, as is matter of daily observation . . . If they arise from an infirm constitution or from some accidental weakness or distemper, they are as in-

nocent as it is to have a weak constitution or a dis-
tempered body.[16]

Wesley observed that there were two kinds of wandering thoughts: those which wandered from God as in
sinful persons or carnal persons and were allowed to
feed the evil disposition in one, which are sinful; and
those which arise from natural causes, and are therefore innocent. The former ones are generally allowed
by the persons, whereas the latter are more or less
uncontrolled until they are taken in hand and brought
into check.

It is the trick of Satan to confuse the sincere, conscientious believer as to which type of thoughts his are.
But an examination of the motives will soon bring to the
surface what they are. If one has such evil thoughts
as feed his pride, gender strife or other forms of evil and
allows them to work in his heart, he may be sure that
their source is evil. But if such thoughts of evil strike
the mind and find there no heart response, even though
the pressure of them upon the mind persist for some
time, one may be sure that their source is not his own
heart-life but they come from some other source.

Sometimes when one is engaged in prayer the mind
will be affected by wandering thoughts to such a degree
as to greatly distract the pray-er. It was Wesley's opinion
as seen in the source just listed that many wandering
thoughts were caused by "evil spirits" which "trouble
even those whom they cannot destroy." It is only to be
expected that he whose delight is to harass the saints
would send his emissaries to disturb the people of God
when in prayer or meditation upon holy things. The
incident of Martin Luther throwing the inkwell at the
devil, who was disturbing him when in prayer and meditation, is well known. An old Methodist minister used
to tell how, when in prayer, he had to battle with
wandering thoughts, he would say to his wandering

thoughts, "Now come on in and sit down here until I'm through praying!"[17]

Wandering thoughts, then, can do one no harm so long as they are held in check properly when one is able to get control of them. One cannot be held morally responsible for those thoughts which he cannot control, as those which may occur in dreams, for example. Sometimes the purest minds have dreams which are unwholesome and occasionally even vile. Take the example of a fine lady who relates the dream experience which recurs ever now and then in which she finds herself engaged in smoking cigarettes. She has never smoked in her life and has never experienced a repressed desire to do so. Occasionally one may dream of immoral conduct and awake shocked and embarrassed. Examination of the past so far as one is able to do so reveals that he has not at any time for one moment entertained any thought of unchastity. Such dreams have no reference to the "filthy dreamers" of Jude 8 and in no way signify an unholy heart. They generally are due to physical tension releases which have no reference to moral conditions whatsoever. Although usually occurring in younger persons, it must not be thought of as shocking if they occur to persons in middle life or beyond. Worrying over such occurrences serves only to heighten the tension in many instances. In some cases, like that of the lady's dream of smoking or those relating to the use of vile language or fighting, worry tends to increase their recurrence. Some psychologists believe that dreams have real significance in relation to some emotional problem of the individual, but this has not been well established. One will do well to disregard most dreams as meaningless fantasies of a wandering mind. It certainly will not do to rely upon them for moral, social, or spiritual guidance. In a very few cases persons have been warned of some impending danger by dreams, and sometimes the unsaved have had dreams which were used to shock them into serious consideration of their need. But to accept them as guidance in matters where decisions of lasting consequence are at stake is folly.

Perhaps a few statements should be made here respecting *infirmities of the body*. In times of physical weakness one is more subject to satanic onslaughts than when in good health. Satan originally used the body as the channel through which he wreaked ruin upon the race in the fall of Adam, and it remains one of his best targets for getting at the person and trapping him again. One has to be on his guard in times of weakness for this reason. The mind tends to be more lax and the body craves certain pampering when in a weakened condition. One is naturally then more vulnerable to the attack of the enemy and less vigilant to throw it off. But it should be remembered that the grace of God is just as strong when we are weak as at any time. "When I am weak, then am I strong," wrote St. Paul. It stands to reason that, if one has served God faithfully in the days of his strength, Christ will not leave him to the mercy of the evil one in his hour of affliction. But one must not become discouraged if there are times of apparent darkness in such times, when the spirit seems to droop and courage lowers. It is no sign of sin nor of letting up spiritually. If one holds on to faith, the light will shine through.

In times of bodily weakness one must also guard his emotions. They often tend to rise and fall with the circumstances surrounding one, and therefore cannot be accepted as a gauge of spiritual conditions. Again, at such times one will often sense the need to cling emotionally to something or someone. Older people especially sense this. This does not mean that one trusts in God less than formerly but may signify merely a sense of feeling the need of greater circumstantial security as age advances. One does not feel as sure of himself as formerly and tends to depend upon others more for sustenance. Sometimes such older persons will feel that they are allowing their weaknesses to be used as an excuse or alibi for not doing what they should for their Lord. And occasionally it must be admitted that Satan strikes a master blow by persuading such persons that they are too old now to take any responsibility; hence they should let up in their prayer life and any other activities which they are actually able to perform. But the Holy Spirit will be faithful to such persons as He always has been and will steer them into the clear channel of His choosing for them. One should not allow Satan to browbeat and condemn him just because the Spirit has chastised him a bit and shown him how he can still be about his Master's business, even if age has taken its toll. Lessened activity does not mean lessened grace in any sense.

A word to younger people who pass through periods of bodily weaknesses may not be amiss here also. In such times there is often the temptation to "take it easy" after one is improved in health and thus to rob the soul of its best hours of meditation and prayer. When in weakness one is forced to relax activity and slow up, there is sometimes the discouraging voice of Satan, accusing one of being out of God's will or this would never have happened to him. Elijah, when under the juniper tree in the desert after being pursued by Jezebel's forces, was anything but the picture of inspiration (I Kings 19). He was ready to give up the task and die, but God had other plans. In either case one cannot afford to listen to the tempter's voice. If Satan cannot get one to succumb to the "take it easy" program and thus rob him of spiritual power, he will then often endeavor to "shove him overboard" into such excessive activities as to break him down again, or rob him of his proper time for soul culture in this way.

Occasionally during times of bodily weaknesses a person in mid-life or younger may experience unusually strong sex urges which must be guarded against also. This is particularly true in cases of hypertension. It is no sign of moral weakness or evil in the heart when such experiences come to one. It is often the need for tension release which creates this condition and it has no moral reference whatsoever.

Whether in youth, mid-life, or old age, one must always reckon with the fact that his body is subject to many infirmities and changing conditions, and that it must be guarded at all times and held in line with his spiritual life, so that he may not be trapped by a misunderstanding of its infirmities or a failure to properly regulate and use its appetites.

CHAPTER XVI

Difficulties with the Emotions

Man's emotional nature is highly essential to his well-being and, when properly understood and controlled, is one of the most outstanding assets of his personality. But when misunderstood, abused, or left without proper development and control, it can become one of the greatest problems of his life, both mentally, physically, and spiritually. The emotions are broadly comprehended in the thought of "feelings," although they go much farther down into human nature than mere feelings. One's emotions actually color large areas of his thinking and in some instances govern many of his most important decisions in life. Unfortunately, far too many young people choose their life's companions largely upon the basis of their emotions. It is little wonder, then, that in so many cases when their emotional outlook upon life changes they become dissatisfied with their choices. Here again much of the failure may be due to the fact that, having made such a choice, they now fail to readjust their changing emotional outlook to the fact of this choice, but further complicate the case by thinking if they could change companions all would be well. But what folly this is! When one realizes that the emotional outlook upon life changes for him with about each decade, think what this would mean if he changed wives or husbands with each changing pattern of emotional outlook!

Now bring this over into the religious life and one can see what apparently happens to many people who fail to realize that they must make an adjustment to this changing emotional pattern. It is perhaps most difficult for children and young people. But being more adaptable they make the adjustment without as much difficulty as older people often have. But young people are not without their problems here.

Take for example the young person who has experienced conversion as a child of five or seven years of age. At twelve or fourteen there is such a complete change in the emotional pattern of life that the child often tends to cast away everything of those earlier days as unbecoming to his now growing-up concepts of life. With this casting away sometimes he confronts his religious experience and there arise in the mind questionings about it. Was it *real?* Did he receive a true "conversion" like older people speak of or was it simply childish faith which blossomed into a belief that he was saved? These questions are sometimes so difficult to face that the person must have reassurance either by another experience similar to it or by the consoling aid of parents or teachers. It is this change which is responsible for so many emotional upsets about everything in children, religion not excluded.

As they progress into the teens, there are other even greater changes which must be faced and coped with. Here again the changing emotional pattern causes them difficulty in making the adjustments necessary and sometimes much questioning of past experiences accompanies it. Even with those young people whose experiences of regeneration and sanctification have been so definite and positive that there can be no doubt about the original experiences, there will still be emotional changes which will demand a new look upon the past experiences and a broadening of the concepts which they originally had. In this process sometimes there occurs such an awakening to new light that the young person is tempted to question whether he really received all he once thought he did in the initial experience. It is at this most critical point in life that youth needs guidance the most from older, settled, and capable persons. Should any young person passing through such an experience read these pages, let him take comfort from the fact that almost all other older people who have started with the Lord early in life have had to make similar readjustments. It is not within the scope of this present work to further discuss such problems, but young readers may find help in another work which has dealt with many such difficulties in youth.[18]

One's emotions play an important role in connection with his religious experience. Sometimes one hears the expression by someone who would remind us of his conservativeness, "Oh, I am not emotional." He means perhaps that he does not give way to or is not governed by his emotions. There is no such thing as an "unemotional" person. Everyone has emotions and everyone expresses emotions, either in a quiet way, a more controlled demonstrative way, or in an explosive manner. Sometimes those persons who deny that they are emotional and act very stolid have more difficulty with their emotions than some who are plainly more extroverts. This is particularly true when anything troubles the person with conservative emotional outlook. He tends to take it to himself, brood over it, turn it over in his mind without expressing it, and attempts to solve it often without the clearer reflection which might be gained by expressing it. Troubles thus tend to become dammed up within his emotions and have no outlet. This may poison one emotionally and so cripple him.

On the other hand, one who is an extreme extrovert and tells his difficulties abroad to everyone may hurt his influence by so doing. He tends to become shallow, dependent upon others, and may in time succumb to complete nervous prostration. Usually extroversion tendencies are characterized by a considerable amount of self-sufficiency and independence, but not always.

In either case one must guard his emotional tendencies and keep them in proper balance. If he does so he may become very stable emotionally. His self-discipline can bring him into the center of the road, where he becomes a more established and balanced person, known as an ambivert. Most people find, however that they tend to revert to either extroversion or introversion tendencies at times. Those who do not think so of themselves have only to inquire of their friends who will be honest with them to come to the truth of this statement. Well has Lincicome said:

> Our feelings are sure to be fluctuating. Fluctuations of emotions obtains in all temperaments. Our life is not built on a level so that we can maintain a constant elevation. We have mountains and valleys and emotional ups and downs. While there is a lot of emotion in religion, yet it is true that our feelings can never be uniform. Our feelings will be like the markets, fluctuating up and down.[19]

One cannot trust his feelings as a guide to his religious experience any more than he can as a guide to health. One may be in good health and yet have downcast feelings, or sometimes one may have poor health and yet have times of very elated feelings. Those who trust their feelings as a gauge of their religious experience are always headed for an up-and-down time of it. Those largely relying upon feelings as the means of evidence of their spiritual state become unstable and cannot be satisfied with their experiences. This reason ought to be plain enough: Feelings are of a nature that never can be satisfied. What pleased them an hour ago may not please them now. They fluctuate because they are governed, not by principle, but by the constantly varying tides of emotional tension within the system. This has to vary with the rhythmical cycles of life itself. Feelings are not anchored to anything moral or spiritual but to the purely biological side of life. Feelings or emotions only take on moral or religious significance when they are channeled into this area of life. It is the will of man directing the emotions which give moral and spiritual tone to them. In themselves one's emotions are purely amoral, like his appetites. One who has known some religious background can drink strong drink, become religiously excited by some service or passing sentiment, and pour forth a flood of emotion tinctured deeply with religious feeling. This has often been demonstrated by certain persons who, when under the influence of drink, could deliver a good talk of religious instruction, with apparent earnestness. The emotional response was there, but the moral and spiritual quality was lacking.

Misguided emotions can become a tragic thing in one's life. There are people who have run on the emotional pattern so long that they have their emotional lives so well set up to follow a certain pattern that they can carry right on through, even religiously, when there is every evidence that they have lost all true and vital religion out of their lives.

One is reminded of the story of the colored church member who was up before the pastor and church board for questioning about his conduct. Said the pastor, "Sam, it am come to us dat you is been stealin' some chickens here in de community. Is dat so?"

"Well, Reverend, I guess dat's so," Sam confessed.

"But you is been takin' a pretty big hand in de meetin', you know, Sam, shoutin' and testifyin' and so on."

"Well, yes, yes, Pastor, dat's so. But I ain't gwine to let no little thing like takin' a few chickens hinder my religion!"

There is imminent and fearful danger ahead for those people who cannot properly relate emotionalism and spiritual life principles. On the one hand, there is the ever-present danger of allowing the absence of emotional elation, such as the feeling of joy or blessing, to become a factor of discouragement whereby doubts are instilled into the mind concerning one's relationship to God, and the soul is hindered. On the other, there is the danger of accepting emotional response as the evidence alone which is necessary for acceptance with God. Neither the one nor the other must be allowed to become the dominant factor, but faith in God through Jesus Christ must ever remain the center repose upon which the soul rests in God.

Wesley, in his sermon on "Satan's Devices," shows how the devil attacks the saints on emotional lines. After pointing out that his first attack is to "damp our joy in the Lord" in his endeavor to "destroy the work of God in the soul," he suggests:

> If he can damp our joy, he will soon attack our peace also. He will suggest, "Are you fit to see God? He is of purer eyes than to behold iniquity. How then can you flatter yourself, so as to imagine that he beholds you with approbation? . . ." More especially in time of sickness and pain he will press this with all his might.[20]

Satan's purpose has ever been to attack people at their weakest spots. The emotions will be subject to rising and falling and to certain other fluctuations such as joy or depression. This provides for him a strong vantage point, especially against those whose emotions have been greatly affected by their religious experiences. And whose have not if he has been truly converted and filled with the Spirit? It would be impossible for a true work of God to be done in the soul and stand over any period of time with proper growth in grace without the emotions being affected.

Hester Ann Rogers, a saintly woman of Wesley's time, relates an experience of hers respecting the depression which she suffered after a severe fever, which serves to illustrate how depressive moods may accompany even the deepest experience of grace. She says, in part:

> A cloud of heaviness has, at some seasons, hung upon my mind; and Satan has taken occasion to suggest, in those times of depression, various accusations of shortcomings

in zeal, activity, and spiritual joy. I do not mean that I was ever left in darkness; no: since I first consciously received a sense of favor with God I never lost it; but within two years last past, I have not always had so clear a witness of perfect love. At other times I have had that witness full and clear. . . . But in nothing else than full salvation, and the witness of it, could my soul ever rest.[21]

In such times of supreme testing of faith one must walk alone by faith. There is at times no sign of sun, moon, or stars in one's emotional heavens and at times for days one must sail by the compass of the Word and faith in the unseen Captain of the soul. But He will do to be trusted. Lady Maxwell once said, "I have often acted faith for sanctification *in the absence of all feeling,* and it has always diffused an indescribable sweetness through my soul."[22]

Speaking of the witness of sanctification, Wesley says:

Indeed, the witness of sanctification is not always clear at first (as neither is that of justification); neither is it afterwards always the same, but, like that of justification, sometimes stronger and sometimes fainter. Yea, and sometimes it is withdrawn. Yet, in general, the latter testimony of the Spirit is both as clear and as steady as the former.[23]

It is well to remember at all times that the work of God stands in the soul, not by emotional overflows of happiness and good feeling, nor even of the realized presence of the Spirit in one's heart, but by faith in Christ and His shed blood alone. The moment one trusts anything other than this, his faith is misplaced and he is on dangerous ground. How comforting to sense the presence of God, and what joy it brings to feel His witness within! But these are not the ground of the work but rather the *results* of it. One should praise God daily for such manifestations of the kindness of God but be prepared to stand by faith alone in the hour of testing when all emotional overflow is absent.

CHAPTER XVII

The Elation-Depression
Cycle Theory

Perhaps an understanding of what this theory has to offer by way of explanations of the emotional nature of man will serve to throw considerable light upon one's emotional experiences in general and their effects upon his religious life in particular.

Life appears to be built quite largely around something of the nature of a cycle. For example, much around us partakes of some form of roundness. The earth's surface is round; the sun, moon, and planets are round and all move in cycles in the universal system. The human body is somewhat round, especially the head. In nature about us rotundity far exceeds any other form. The trees with their round trunks, the flowers, and even many stones speak to us of rotundity. The bodies of animals and fishes and fowls likewise partake of something of this nature. And what would civilization do without the "wheel" in its myriad forms? One wonders as he looks at all this if there may not be something in the nature of mankind which partakes of the cycle nature. Could it be that man's mind operates somewhat in cycles? That his emotions are subject to rises and falls no one could dispute for a moment. In all this surrounding there must be some place for the idea that the emotions of mankind are governed by something of the nature of the cycle.

Psychologists have quite well established the fact of elation-depression cycles in the emotional and mental behavior of both normal and abnormal persons. This is essentially an emotion or "feeling" cycle. It governs much in the average person's life and goes far toward establishing definite behavior patterns in both normal and abnormal persons. Some persons are shocked to learn that there is no such thing as a "normal" person, psychologically speaking. All persons are subject to emotional patterns which at times are either above or below normal. Normalcy is merely a standard of emotional and mental behavior pattern somewhere between two extremes. This standard is arrived at by selecting the largest number of persons whose behavior is somewhere between these two extremes as the norm. But any person may temporarily swing out of these bounds and return without being considered abnormal. It is when one swings out too far either in an elation or a depression cycle and remains there too long a time at once that his behavior is said to become abnormal. And there must also be considered the height of the elation cycle or the depth of the depression cycle. Milder forms of either cycle may persist for considerable lengths of time without damage to the emotional or mental health. It is the more violent cases, or those in which the elation cycle is much higher or the depression cycle is much deeper than is normal, which are considered as abnormal.[24]

In cases where the elation cycle reaches a point at which the patient loses control of himself in hysterical laughter or crying for long periods, or the depression cycle extends downward to the point that one becomes so excessively morbid as to refuse to speak to others or secludes himself over long periods, the person has definitely become abnormal and needs psychiatric care. Often in the beginning phases of such behavior patterns a relative or friend, a minister or doctor who knows how to help the patient can pull him out of this condition before it progresses to its worst stages. The person can be made to see that he is giving away to something which will finally drive him to its farthest extreme, and by his self-control of his emotions he can save himself from being pushed into the extreme state. There are cases, however, where the disorder is deeper than average and cannot be controlled by the person himself without expert psychiatric care. We shall not attempt to deal with this form of the extreme but rather with the more normal elation-depression cycles to which all persons are subject.

It is apparent, then, that most persons have somewhat noticeable elation-depression cycles which extend throughout their lives. In most people this pattern appears to vary but little after adulthood patterns are established, especially until mid-life, when it may be upset for a while due to the bodily changes taking place in both men and women, after which it may return to its former pattern for the rest of life, until extreme age is reached. In other cases the cycles become more pronounced in adulthood and continue to be so throughout life. In persons who have come to understand these cycles and control them, they are not noticeable to other persons.

The elation-depression cycles run the whole gamut of human emotions. They range all the way from the slightest elation, producing only a warm, inward good feeling of cheerfulness, to the mildest depression, sometimes referred to as "the blues," on the mild level, to the extremes described above where the person is said to become abnormal. Only a few persons, however, ever experience the extremes. One should not allow this to worry him nor should he fear that he may become abnormal any more that one should worry about the pleasant matter of eating producing ulcers in the stomach. It is a normal condition of the emotions in which there appears to be a "swing" from the cheerful to the more serious moods of life. A few persons experience very sudden swings of the emotional pattern which are noticeable to their friends. All persons experience these swings in varying degrees but not so evidently as to become readily noticeable to others. These cycles in themselves are essential to the welfare of personality just as digestion is to the body. It is only when the cycles get out of proper balance that they need our special attention—just as excessive acid in the stomach may disturb the digestive function.

It is apparent, however, that far too few people understand this elation-depression cycle of their emotional behavior pattern and for that reason cannot understand what is happening to them when the cycles swing a bit toward the extremes. For instance, here is a person who has had his emotional ups and downs, days when he was extra cheerful and others when the world did not look quite so bright, but he took it all in good stride. Then for no apparent reason he passes into a clouded period when the sunshine of elation does not appear for several days. He becomes depressed and cannot understand why he feels so low in spirit. The world looks dark and foreboding and the future takes on a gloomy appearance. He wonders if he is sick, but there are no physical ailments bothering him. Finally, things take a turn for the better and he becomes more cheerful, life becomes bright, and all is well again. He can assign no more reason for the improvement which seemed spontaneous than for the onset of the gloomy period. This may be followed by weeks or months of sunny living before another "gloomy period" sets in. Other persons find these emotional ups and downs are shorter periods and more frequent than this, but the reaction to them is similar in most cases.

When one brings all this over into the religious life it may be seen immediately that one's religious-emotional life will be affected by it. It will become apparent that its connection with faith and "feelings" religiously cannot be separated from one's life. If properly understood it should provide no more difficulty than does a case of indigestion in respect to one's faith in God and his religious experiences. But only a few have this understanding of their emotional problems with respect to religious life. This may be largely due, first, to the lack of understanding of the emotional patterns of life in general; and second, to the misconception that when one is fully trusting in God, and especially when one is filled with the Spirit, there should be a constancy of joy and an inner calm of undisturbed peace. This misconception has taken root largely from the fact that the preaching of full salvation has so often been accompanied with expressions of the joy and peace which it brings, without the explanation that this "joy and peace" are not to be found in the realm of changing human emotions, but deep within the spiritual nature of man.

It is to be regretted that too much preaching upon the *resultant life* of the Spirit-filled believer has been directed to the emotional rather than the spiritual and ethical nature of man. In consequence of this there has grown up among believers a sort of hallowed respect for the "good feelings" which accompany the Spirit's baptism and these have been made the test for the continued approbation of God and the Spirit's witness, much to the detriment of the whole work of God in the soul. One is not to stand in God's sight upon whether or not he "feels" the presence of God, but in the faith of the Lord Jesus Christ. The *witness of the Spirit* does not stand in any human feeling, but in a *deep, inner moral and spiritual consciousness* that "I, even I, am reconciled to God," to quote Wesley,[25] and that "the blood of Jesus Christ his Son cleanseth us [*me*] from all sin" (I John 1:7).

It is true that this witness of the Spirit will break forth into emotional overflows of joy which will affect the natural emotions many times. But these may rise and fall for no apparent reason, and one cannot rest his faith in God for salvation upon any such transient conditions. It should be remembered that it is quite possible that one will not be "feeling good" the day he dies! Certainly the Lord Jesus may come to us with great blessing in this hour; God grant that He may! But should it not be so, one will find then that faith alone will carry him to the bosom of the Saviour in paradise.

Mark Guy Pearse well remarks on the point of feelings:

> *There is no great virtue in happy feeling.* I do not know that I could be more confident of a man's honesty because he assured me that he felt happy; or that I could rely upon his word with more assurance on that account. . . .[26]

Look into Westminster Abbey and read there the memorials of mighty men, or visit Arlington Cemetery and read the epitaphs there. Did these people feel happy when bullets whined by them, cannon balls burst near them; in Arctic's cold or Africa's heat; or in privation, sorrow, and even martyrdom for the sake of Christ's cause? No! They were not doing this for mere happiness or good feeling, but because a cause worthy of devotion and even death was at stake. They were motivated, not by transient feeling and sentiment, but by far deeper, nobler, and holier means.

To return to our elation-depression cycle problem, it must be further observed that one may be going along smoothly and feeling that all is well in his spiritual life when almost all of a sudden he passes under a cloud. This depression may grow deeper and last for several days or even weeks in some cases. The spirit droops, the outlook is gloomy, and it seems that every attempt to break through it in prayer or meditation is met with a heaviness and rebuff. Satan appears and points an accusing finger. One searches his heart and looks over the recent past but cannot find where he has broken his covenant with God. Or it may be that Satan has gotten the advantage of him in some small thing which he did or said just before the onset of the depression, which now rises like some fearful nightmare to taunt him under Satan's guise as an "angel of light." His faith and patience will be sorely tried, for he cannot understand why this depression should continue to hold him in its merciless grip. But there seems nothing he can do but to endure, "as seeing him who is invisible." Then, finally, the sun breaks through and he is again in a mood of joyfulness and praise. He may be unable to assign any specific reason for which he came out of this depressive cycle. There was no more extra praying that day than any day before. The cloud passed away for no more apparent reason than it had appeared at first.

One may retire for the night in a good mood spiritually speaking and even drift off to slumber in a spirit of prayer. Upon rising the next morning a weight of heaviness is upon him and he finds prayer most difficult. The reading of the Word holds out little help or light and there is no desire to even attempt to sing. He has overnight exchanged the song of joy for the garment of mourning, so to speak. Tears may fill the eyes for no apparent reason, except the "lonely feeling" of heaviness. And men as well as women may at times experience this. At such times one may be gripped by a sudden fear for the well-being of a distantly located relative or close friends, or a feeling of insecurity about himself or his possessions. Often to fight these feelings the hardest does not relieve the condition and the struggle in prayer seems futile. In such times the suggestion of Satan that God has forgotten to be gracious or that for some unknown reason there has come a breach between the soul and its Redeemer may roll over one like a heavy fog descending from a mountainside. One should rest implicitly upon the promises of God and the shed blood of Christ and refuse to question either God's mercy or his own experience. The cycle of depression will pass away as readily as it came and one will see in the light afterward that he was in no way out of harmony with God.

There are times of elation, likewise, which are as spontaneous as the times of depression. But since these are so much more to our liking for life and bring joyfulness with them, one does not notice them as being anything out of the ordinary as he does the depression cycle. One may arise in the morning feeling unusually cheerful. The day glides by smoothly and everything is cheerful. Even the little things which would sometimes be annoying are not noticeable. Prayer is easy and reading is a delight. One is borne along upon a current of happiness which lifts him far above the surroundings and makes him feel as if he were almost at heaven's vestibule. It is relatively easy to speak to another about the things of God, and the opportunity to witness for Christ is taken so much easier than sometimes. Life is bright and cheerful and the future is filled with promise. Yet when one stops to examine it all—but who does then!—he finds that he has not prayed much if any extra, nor given himself to other religious exercises more than in times of depression, perhaps not as much. He has not especially laid himself out in spiritual exercises that he should be so blessed. It is a token of God's special favor to him and he enjoys it to the full. Perhaps he does not realize that, along with all the spiritual blessings, he is really riding the crest of an elation cycle which makes all of life easier and brighter. Normally, the elation cycle is much longer than the depression cycle, which accounts for the happier mood of most people. But those whose depression cycle is longer than average should refuse to become alarmed by this. It is only a normal condition with them. It may, indeed, be shortened by a better understanding of it and a better control of themselves when passing through it.

No attempt is being made here in any way whatsoever to show that much of what one normally thinks of as the blessing of God may be accounted for by the rise and progress of the emotional elation cycle. Far from it, for the least amount of the "blessing" of God can in no wise be accounted for in this way. No amount of human elation can take the place of the Spirit's blessing to our hearts. But just as Satan may accompany our gloom cycle with accusations and testings (which God permits for the trial of our faith and His glory), so the Holy Spirit may accompany our elation cycle with His delights and joys. But more than this: In the midst of the depression cycle with all its unpleasantness and in the absence of all human elation one can be conscious of the "joy of the Lord," which is far deeper rooted in the soul than mere human elation. And in the height of the crest of human emotional elation there is often present in the heart of the saint of God a sense of burden or sadness for those who are out of Christ. In other words, these emotional factors of human experience are matters with which one must reckon but they do not control the matters of grace and Christian experience in the soul.

The next time the train starts through a tunnel of depression one should reckon with that fact and keep his seat. Life is made up of depressive, somber days and elated, sunny periods. One is essentially just as spiritual when trusting God alone in times of "gray, dark days" as in the sunshine of abundant joy. There are joys and sorrows, mountains and valleys, heights and depths in the spiritual life as well as in the emotional life, and the one is bound to be affected by the other, so far as sensations and emotional responses go. But these must not control the life, but rather they must be controlled by faith in God and a life of ethical practices in keeping with this faith. The saying of an older brother in Christ whom we knew in youth is pertinent here, "Circumstances never enter into grace, but grace often enters into circumstances." If one will allow all his emotional problems to be controlled by the rule of that faith which "endured, as seeing him who is invisible" (Heb. 11:27), and the grace which God so graciously provides, he will come out all right in the end. It has been in the belief that many need a better understanding of their emotional problems and with the hope that the solutions here offered would be helpful that so much space has been given to this elation-depression cycle theory. It is not claimed that all one's emotional problems may be solved by the application of this theory; far from it. But that there are many areas in which an understanding of one's emotions and the proper application of this knowledge to his emotional and religious problems would prove helpful, none can well doubt.

Chapter XVIII

Distinguishing Between
Human and Carnal Traits

There is hardly an area of the Spirit-filled life where some people have had more difficulty than in this one. This is especially true of those persons who by nature have a very hypersensitive personality or are high-tensioned emotionally. It is the purpose here to examine certain traits which, while they may be purely human on the one hand, may likewise partake of the carnal element on the other; and to determine as nearly as possible under what circumstances the manifestation would be likely to be merely human and under what conditions it may be carnal. This is a delicate task to set before ouselves and it is not claimed that the results will be satisfactory to everyone reading the deductions. But since it is an area of considerable problem to many, it is certainly worth the endeavor to try to reach as nearly a satisfactory explanation as one can, within the limits of so widely varying experiences of different personalities and various opinions as to what constitutes a carnal trait. There is not so great a difference of opinion as to what constitutes a carnal trait as there is as to what manifestations are evidences of the unsanctified carnal nature, and what are merely manifestations of human nature under stress or test.

We may begin with *fear*. When is fear natural and when is it carnal? There are three kinds of fear referred to in the Bible: filial fear, natural fear, and carnal fear. Every justified and sanctified person loves God with filial fear. "The fear of the Lord is the beginning of wisdom" (Ps. 111:10). When John says, "He that feareth is not made perfect in love" because "perfect love casteth out fear" (I John 4:18), he does not mean this filial fear. We are exhorted to "stand in awe, and sin not" (Ps. 4:4). Nor does he refer to natural or constitutional fear, such as the fear of a bear, or of wicked men harming one, or even of darkness. This is a native element of our constitution and is for our protection. Timidity or shyness is part of this element of fear and is not to be consigned to a place with carnal fear. Many a Spirit-filled person has experienced great timidity when called to witness for Christ in a strange place, or when duty demanded him to sing or speak under new or different circumstances. Nor is the dread of meeting some outstanding person a sign of carnal fear, or to go to some place where one realizes that physical violence could come to him. A thousand fears may be perfectly consistent with perfect love.

What, then, is "carnal fear"? Baldwin has defined it thus:

> Spiritual fear, as we have called it, for want of a better name, is servile dread of the Almighty, slavish fear of men, carnal shrinking from showing one's colors, shrinking from doing one's duty because of the consequences, or any other form of fear that hinders a man from being his whole bigness for God and from standing in every place where brave men are needed.[7]

This carnal fear is that inward drawing back from taking up the cross and going all the way with the Master; that drawing back with lack of faith, fearing that to take up the cross and shun the world will bring persecution, which the soul is not willing to bear for Christ. It is that dread of the presence of God because there is the inward realization that one is not ready to meet Him in perfect peace. One may even stand in awe and examine his experience in God's presence with a sort of trusting fear without being at the same time carnal. This fear is in the hearts of those who "draw back," in whose souls the Lord has said He would "have no pleasure."

Much has been said in preaching and writing about *anger* as a carnal trait, and there is considerable confusion in some minds as to when it is or is not. Some, indeed, have gone so far as to leave the impression that all anger is carnal. But this cannot be true, for God himself is said to be angry at times. Jesus looked around upon the crowd with anger upon one occasion because of the hardheartedness in them (Mark 3:5).

There are two kinds of anger: carnal anger and righteous indignation or anger against wickedness. Perhaps it will be well to mention the latter first. Sometimes parents become angry and need to punish the disobedient child for his welfare when the parental authority has been challenged by disobedience. This is not necessarily carnal. There is a righteous anger against such disobedience which the parent should have. This arises, not out of a sense of vengeance, but out of grief and disappointment that the child should so challenge the authority of the parent. The infliction of punishment is not done with any sense of pleasure but with regret that it must be done. The carnal parent is likely to experience carnal anger mixed with the emotion of parental anger at such times. But in the heart of the sanctified there is nothing but righteous anger against the evil in the child and the desire to correct him for his own good. This will often take the form of stern measures and sometimes strong words but never a vengeful attitude. There are parents who feel that they cannot punish their children sternly lest they lose their sanctification. In the matter of discipline, parents must realize that sanctification is not spineless, and vigorous discipline of children is a holy exercise if done with pure motives.

Righteous indignation is something which must be handled with great care even in the most mature Christian, lest it border upon carnal wrath. When God cleanses the heart from the carnal nature, it is evident that He does not remove from it the ability to manifest anger, for this would be to "de-nature" the very human constitution. God removes nothing essentially human from us in cleansing our natures from inbred or native sin. The possibility of becoming again contaminated with sin is ever present but becomes a reality only when one willfully sins by act of disobedience and thus again pollutes his nature, as Adam did at the beginning. Herein is the danger everyone must constantly face, inherent in the very principle of freedom itself.

We may describe righteous indignation as that holy zeal against unrighteousness in action or attitude on the part of another, whoever he may be. This may take the form of spoken words or actions against such an evil deed, but the motive behind such must ever be the glory of God by our standing against that which is evil. It is a form of holy hatred against sin, but it can never for an instant possess the smallest amount of hatred for the offending person or persons. It is the evil against which this righteous zeal must be manifested and not the person manifesting it. For example, one sees a big bully of a man tackle a little, weakly man or a boy for no just cause whatsoever, and take every advantage of him, beating him unmercifully. There will arise in the heart of a holy man an intense feeling that here is gross injustice which should be immediately stopped. If the man is able to do so, he may rush to the scene and intervene on behalf of the weaker person, trying to protect him in whatever way he can. Plainly, his feelings of protest against this thing will be stirred to the depths. But he will experience no carnal anger, for he has no evil feelings against the big man as a man, but against the wicked principle which he is manifesting. When it is over, there will be no rancor of ill will against the offending man, and the same man would not hesitate to do a good deed for him if he were in need.

Many people have difficulty in distinguishing carnal anger from natural responses to shock, insult, injury, and the like and are often in bondage to this constant questioning in their minds. Some have this difficulty to the point that they almost cast away their confidence and doubt at times whether or not they are fully cleansed from sin. And yet these same persons have such a clear witness to perfect love at other times that they cannot doubt but what the work has been done in their hearts. What is the answer to this problem?

Perhaps it will be necessary to approach the answer to this question from several angles. It may be observed that there is a considerable difference in the constitutional make-up of different individuals, which accounts for much difference as to how one responds to various emotional stimuli; and further, that the condition in any individual may vary with his changing physical condition, as has been pointed out by Wright:

> In recent years much has come to light about the influence of glands upon man, and here we see the close linkage between the physical and the mental. Under-activity of the thyroid gland, for example, makes for slowness of movement and slowness of understanding. Over-activity makes for high tension and drive. Over-secretion of the pituitary seems to be linked with courage and initiative, while under-secretion is linked with lassitude and timidity.[28]

This may well account for the fact that the high-tension person will react to shock or injury far quicker than the low-tension person, and for the fact also that at some times one may be much more susceptible to such quick reaction than at others.

Wesley observed:

> One may start, tremble, change color, or be otherwise disordered in body, while the soul is calmly stayed on God and remains in perfect peace. Nay, the mind itself may be deeply distressed, may be exceeding sorrowful, may be

> perplexed and pressed down by heaviness and anguish, even to agony, while the heart cleaves to God by perfect love and the will is wholly resigned to Him.[29]

Perhaps it will be permissible here for the author to relate an experience of boyhood days which well illustrates the point we are endeavoring to clear up here. I had been in Bible college and received much new light concerning the matter of full sanctification. But I had not yet received my own experience of the Spirit's baptism after prolonged groaning and mortification as some others had. With limited light I plunged in by faith and received it with a flood of overflowing joy.

However I was greatly troubled because my experience was not accompanied by the same reactions that others talked about. In this frame of mind there began at times to arise doubts as to whether my experience had been genuine as others, and yet there was the ever-recurring witness of the Spirit that the work was done. But in this time of testing, one day a young lad in the school slipped up behind me unaware and, leaping upon my back, nearly knocked me down to the pavement. Instantly there was a hot flash ran all over my body, followed by a sudden jerking of my arms and releasing of myself from the boy and a sharply spoken word requesting that he not do this again.

The lad bounded off, laughing at his prank, while I mounted the stairs to my dormitory room and fell upon my knees in great agony of spirit. There I wept and prayed, wrestled with the question of whether or not this was an outburst of carnal anger, and over the whole question of my sanctification. After a considerable while there came into my heart a quiet peace and assurance that all was well.

For several years this incident stood out in memory and I often wondered just what took place. Later, upon a further enlightenment as to the human personality and its functions, especially those of the nervous system, it was all made plain. What really occurred was this: When the lad leaped upon the writer's back, there was a complete shock to the nervous system. The brain immediately went into action. The central nervous system was notified to fortify the body for a possible fall. It in turn speeded up the heart tremendously, which in turn shot a heavy load of adrenalin into the system. This toned up every muscle necessary for the fortification and sent the blood coursing through the veins faster and more profusely. As a result there was flashed to the skin surface more blood, changing both the heat and color of the skin temporarily. The muscles became tensed up and went into reflexive action without any further direction from the will whatsoever. The brain speeded up its motor activity, and quick speech was thereby produced without conscious effort on the part of the will.

All this took place in a few seconds, resulting in the hot flash felt, the quick response of the muscles in getting the boy released from the body, and the quickly spoken words of warning not to repeat the act. The words were not biting nor harsh but merely self-defensive; and when the episode was over there was no malice or ill will, and no feeling of resentment whatsoever. What happened? The nervous system simply responded normally to a sudden shock and that was all there was to it. There was no carnal anger present. The reason for the question about that in the first place was the former questionings of the mind relative to the spiritual state, of which Satan made capital stock when this misunderstood activity of the body took place.

This episode has been related and explained at length to help explain the nature of a shock to the body and its response to it. The shock may come from physical injury, social insult, sudden surprises, or any of many different sources and the resulting reaction may follow a similar pattern. One should not be surprised at such reactions because they are perfectly normal and are not the result of sin in the heart but of our broken and infirm bodies. The main thing in every such situation is to know that the love of God has been made perfect in the soul by the cleansing Blood at some time in the past and that one's consecration and faith are up-to-date. This is not an explanation intended to defend those who have explosions of carnal anger. In most such cases there is little or no doubt in the mind but what the manifestation was carnal anger.

We have sometimes pointed out that there is another way in which to test any such reaction to a situation in which one questions whether there was carnal anger present. After the episode has passed, examine the test tube of the emotions, motives, and leftover attitude about the whole affair. If one finds that there remains in the spirit a rankling, self-defensive attitude of resentment against the person, which, if opportunity afforded, would be used to square matters with him, put him in his place, put one's self in the best light at his expense, or the like—one may rest assured that there was carnal anger present. Carnal anger is selfish and bears evil resentment against the person involved, or the thing or object which aroused the anger. If one can look into his emotional test tube and see there nothing but pure love, nothing which would work "ill to his neighbour," naught but the settlings of a temporarily distraught nervous system, then he can be sure it was a mere shock and that no carnal anger was present.

Human experience is much like this, for those who have been cleansed from the bondage of their former corruptions. The reactions of the old carnal nature set up certain emotional patterns in the personality which are not entirely erased with the removal of the carnal nature. The carnal nature, after all, is not a sort of addition to our humanity but rather a principle of sinful disposition by which the natural elements of our nature were warped out of proper shape and put to evil usages. Therefore when it is cleansed, nothing essentially human is removed, but only the evil principle which used the elements of personality wrongly is taken away. For this reason there may be at times certain physical reactions which seem to follow the pattern of the former carnal reactions, but which in reality are not carnal because the motive and principle from which they come are no longer carnal.

One of the strongest biological urges is the sex urge. This is in itself perfectly harmless and sinless. To feel the sense of need for sexual fulfillment, as most every normal single young person does, is nothing but natural. So long as the motives and desires of a person are controlled by proper means, and his thoughts kept properly governed, this appetite can be no more harm to him than the appetite for food.

Courting couples sometimes feel the sense of sex urges deeply within them, and married couples who must be separated oftentimes feel the sense of this biological hunger much more keenly. These urges are native and not sinful. Nor is their presence in any sense the sign of sinful "lust." St. Paul said, "I had not known lust, except the law had said, Thou shalt not covet" (Rom. 7:7). Now to "lust" in the Biblical sense of the word is to desire to secure something illegally or illegitimately. "Thou shalt not covet . . . any thing that is thy neighbour's" (Exod. 20:17). The native surge of biological hunger in single or married persons under certain circumstances is no more lustful than is the hunger for food. It is when this urge is allowed to become a "desire" directed toward an illegitimate object that it becomes lust.

Now a desire is a desire only when it becomes an act of the will. This is the sense in which lust is to be Biblically understood. During times when a sense of biological sex urge is present Satan may appeal to the mind with suggestions for its satisfaction, which constitute a temptation. But if this is rejected and one refuses to consider it, it can be no harm to him. Before the purified soul can become guilty of lust the person must accept the suggestion and allow the unholy desire for illegal gratification to be set up in his heart. The pressure of Satan can sometimes be so great that one can resist such thoughts only with the aid of the Holy Spirit and prayer; but when they have passed, he is assured of heart purity because there was not within him any wish or desire to yield one iota to Satan's suggestions. Even if the imagination has been played upon during the fight with the enemy and the physical appetite strongly appealed to, there has been no lust so long as the will has not capitulated to the suggestion and allowed "desire" to become a *willful* act of the mind. When one is on this territory he treads dangerous ground, but he is as safe as his will to refrain from all sin, and as the grace of God to keep him in such an hour. Sometimes afterward Satan will point the accusing finger, but he has no ground upon which to stand when the will has been unrelenting in its vigil against evil. And this applies to every form of sin.

Section Four

Dangers of the Spirit-filled Life

Wherefore let him that thinketh he standeth take heed lest he fall. There hath no temptation taken you but such as is common to man: but God is faithful, who will not suffer you to be tempted above that ye are able; but will with the temptation also make a way to escape, that ye may be able to bear it (I Cor. 10:12-13).

Therefore we ought to give the more earnest heed to the things which we have heard, lest at any time we should let them slip (Heb. 2:1).

Watch and pray, that ye enter not into temptation: the spirit indeed is willing, but the flesh is weak (Matt. 26:41).

CHAPTER XIX

Temptations to Doubt

The Spirit-filled life is beset with many dangers along the way. If Satan cannot keep one in sin and ruin him, he will set about what means he may devise for crippling his usefulness in the way of righteousness, thus hindering both his progress toward the Holy City and his influence to win others. As one has well warned:

> The experience of sanctification has its peculiar dangers . . . It is the main business of satanic powers, often using human means as their instruments, to wreck the sanctified life. If the temptation to sin does not avail, an attempt is frequently made along the line of religion by forcing the soul to unreasonable extremes, seeking to turn faith into presumption and faithfulness into fanaticism. An example of this is to be found in our Lord's wilderness temptation.[1]

It will be the purpose in this section to point out what are considered the major dangers confronting those who walk this way of faith. Those who are not yet in the experience often imagine that when they are Spirit-filled their trials will largely be over and their way to heaven filled only with joy and delight. But the trials of the Spirit-filled are often more keenly felt than those of the justified. This is partly due to the fact that their nature is now more spiritually sensitive and partly because Satan now recognizes in them an even greater enemy of his cause. The unsanctified have more inward trials with the carnal nature; the sanctified have more outward trials and battles of faith. But the Spirit-filled person has a greater armor with which to fight the enemy and no inward "fifth columnist" to betray him while he fights. The fact remains that there is still a fight to the finish against the enemy.

One of the early dangers which the Spirit-filled may experience is the temptation to doubt concerning his experience of heart purity. Of faith John Fletcher said:

> Herein lies the grand mistake of many poor but precious souls: they are afraid to believe lest it be *presumption,* because they have not yet comfort, love, joy, etc., not considering that this is to look for fruit before the tree is planted.[2]

And another has pointed out an important point in this matter:

> The temptations to doubt concerning one's purity are much more intricate and perplexing than those regarding the forgiveness of sins. The most holy and devoted persons are more frequently compelled to approach the cleansing blood by faith,—for the *evidence* of purity than for that of pardon.[3]

The reason for this is not far to seek: the forgiveness of sins is accompanied by such a great *outward* change, and the inward change is likewise so great from sin to grace, that the witness of this is always partially self-evident.

On the other hand, the inward work of cleansing is so delicately poised in the soul and the fine line so often drawn between the carnal and the human traits of human nature is so close as to be difficult for many to distinguish. It is readily apparent that many would find it difficult to always have a perfectly certain assurance of this cleansing being an accomplished fact. Add to this the often taught opinion that one may lose his state of sanctification without losing his experience of justification, and it will be seen again why some are more easily confused.

Furthermore, it must be kept in mind that some have had a far more outstanding experience of regeneration than they did of sanctification. The emotional shock sustained in their lives from this experience is far beyond that which they received in sanctification. This order is reversed in the case of others whose regenerated experience was not nearly so profound as their experience of the Spirit's baptism. This second crisis in this case proves to be so outstanding that it can never be questioned.

It was Wesley's opinion that there were very few who received the witness of complete assurance to their sanctification at first but who needed to have it reaffirmed to them by the Spirit several times before they became established fully in it. Of temptation to doubt he said.

> In the hour of temptation Satan clouds the work of God and injects various doubts and reasonings, especially in those who have either very weak or very strong understandings. At such times there is absolutely need of that witness, without which the work of sanctification not only could not be discerned, but could no longer subsist . . . In these circumstances, therefore, a direct testimony that we are sanctified is necessary in the highest degree.[4]

It is evident from this and reference to John Fletcher's experience respecting heart purity that it was believed among early Methodists that one may lose the experience of sanctification by doubting and casting away his confidence without losing his state of regeneration. On this point Brengle comments:

> The Rev. John Fletcher, who Mr. Wesley thought was the holiest man who had lived since the days of the Apostle John, lost the Blessing five times before he was finally established in the grace of Holiness, and Mr. Wesley declared that he was persuaded, from his observations, that people usually lost the Blessing several times before they learned the secret of keeping it.[5]

It is much more likely for younger persons who are susceptible to much new light, or those sanctified very soon after regeneration, to have difficulty in becoming established in the grace of the Spirit's fullness than for those who after considerable experience have sought and found this fullness as the solution to their problem with the carnal mind. They are usually more mature and their seeking is with greater light. However, one cannot discount the maturity nor the light of such persons as Mr. Fletcher. And many others who have been fully cleansed in earlier life have had hard-fought battles with Satan concerning their state of heart purity in later years. Unfortunately, some do not seem to apprehend fully the difference between the pressure of Satan tempting to doubt and the actual fact of doubting. This temptation is not like that to outward sin, where the allurement is set before one, but is an inward pressure sometimes giving rise to an inward feeling of questionings. The believer does not yield to this suggestion, throw up his hands, and say, "All is lost." But the subtle insinuation of the devil later is to the effect that one had questions in his mind. Of course it may be so; but why? Did not the archfiend himself put them there? And is a soul, however holy, responsible for questions which another raises in the mind?

Sometimes ministers state that their assurance of full salvation is so great that they would not "thank an angel" to come and tell them they are wholly the Lord's. Well and good; if they would not, there are millions of others who would! And if one could take a peep behind the scenes at this same person, sometimes he may find him in a mood in which he would not exactly object to a bit of angelic reassurance. It is certainly folly for anyone to do as some have done when at the place of prayer, seeking the assurance of cleansing, or even pardon, when they vow, "Lord, I will never doubt Thee again!" One may be forced to retract this statement or be found wanting in truthfulness about it later in life. God does not wish us to tie ourselves with a lot of unreasonable promises. All He wants is our full self-giving, the entire life laid down for Him, and our faith placed in Him completely. There is nothing which will take the place of this, no matter how much we may promise.

It should also be born in mind that to question one's experience and to doubt God are two entirely different things. Too few people recognize this difference but it is a vast one. Few conscientious souls ever doubt God or His loving-kindness or His work in the soul. It is merely the question as to whether one is wholly given to God, and, therefore, fully approved by Him. It should further be said that to question one's experience and seek God's reassuring witness does not in any wise destroy one's experience. It is only when one repudiates the work of God in the soul by disclaiming it that his experience is lost. Even then when the soul is sincerely in deep questionings it is not likely that God withdraws His Spirit from him.

Thomas Cook warned about temptation in the following words:

> It is a mistake to suppose that there is any state of grace this side of heaven which puts a Christian where he is exempt from temptation. So long as a soul is on probation it will be tempted by solicitations to sin . . . The struggle with the flesh, or inbred sin, or depravity by whatever name it may be called, comes to an end when all antagonisms to God are expelled from the soul and Christ reigns without a rival. But there are other enemies than those which exist within, against whom we shall have to fight strenuously to the end.[6]

Temptation is normal to all degrees of grace and only serves to strengthen the believer if steadfastly resisted. But one must be always on the alert for the enemy and ward off his suggestions before they are allowed to develop into a desire to try them out or discouragement, which may lead to disaster.

Brockett has left a note of warning about the possibility of losing this grace of Christian holiness which needs to be sounded, for although when cleansed from sin one stands a far better chance of never backsliding, it is always a possibility:

> The doctrine of entire sanctification by faith maintains the even balance of the truth as between God's sovereign grace on the one hand and human responsibility on the other. The believer in entire sanctification by faith acknowledges, therefore, like the Apostle Paul, that, as an individual, it is possible for him to suffer solemn and final loss, I Cor. 9:29.[7]

While the subject of temptation is being considered it may be wise to pass on here the warning of T. M. Anderson about vow-making, upon which we touched briefly above. His words are so apt that we shall submit them without comment:

> Mistakes are often made in moments of religious fervor and zeal, which prove afterward to be sources of trouble to the sanctified. Vows and promises are made at such times with the purest of intentions; but when later they find these cannot be fulfilled because of certain limitations within themselves, they become a prey to the devil's accusations. Besides this their conscience, because of their lack of knowledge, will condemn them.[8]

We must conclude, then, that so long as we remain in the flesh and have to contend with the devil, even the best of saints will be subjected to times when their integrity will be called into question by him.

Chapter XX

Danger of Leanness of Soul

There is the ever-present danger of soul leanness which the Spirit-filled believer must face and overcome. The inward man must be "renewed day by day." One cannot receive sufficient grace at an altar of prayer to carry him through to the end of his journey.

While God does not withdraw His Spirit from one for every slight provocation, it is evident that if one continues to allow the "cares of this life" to pile up in his way and hinder the progress of his growth and his devotional life from being constantly enriched he will thereby so deprive his spiritual nature of the necessary nurture that it will die of sheer leanness. One can starve his spiritual nature the same as he can his physical nature. Soul culture is quite as important to the well-being of one's spiritual life as physical food and exercise are to his physical life.

In times of hurry and bustle such as these, entirely too many religious people are depending upon a brief morning or evening devotional period and the help they receive in the Sunday worship services to take care of all their souls' need. This may be sufficient to keep alive a sickly and anemic experience of grace in the soul but it will never develop a stalwart Christian character.

If one is to "grow in grace, and in the knowledge of our Lord and Saviour Jesus Christ," he must of necessity have seasons of private communion with God. There are many things which demand the attention of private soul culture in prayer and meditation which cannot in the very nature of the case be cared for in public, not even in public family worship. No one ever developed a great mind or enlarged soul who did not find time for private seasons of prayer and meditation.

No scientist or inventor ever discovered or invented anything of value in public. It was alone in the quiet meditation that he unlocked the secret and brought to light the usefulness of the thing heretofore unrealized. Great characters are likewise not molded in the public but in the hours of reflection, meditation, and self-development which are spent alone with one's self. Likewise, there can be no truly deep and lasting development of piety apart from the secret chamber of prayer, devotion, and self-examination. Those who attempt to build up a piety without this method succeed in building only a thin veneer of the real thing. Then they so many times wonder why it "cracks" under the test. An inch board of solid oak may swell after a little rain has hit it but it will hold together, whereas a light oak veneer will often crack right open. It is in the times of deep devotion alone with God that abiding convictions are developed and the strength to carry them into action is received.

Another weakness among Spirit-filled people today is the fact that far too few "give attendance to reading," as Paul exhorted Timothy to do. A few verses or a chapter now and then in the Word and a hurried glance at the Sunday school lesson are often the extent of many people's reading for weeks at a time, so far as spiritually helpful literature goes. Secular books and magazines are allowed far too much prominence. Wesley observed that a reading people would be a growing people, and it is only to the extent that people inform their minds about the things of God that they can be expected to grow in this knowledge. A full heart and an empty head paves the way for fanaticism or other false enthusiasms, while a full head and a cold heart heads one straight for formalism in religion. One must counterbalance the other. Just as the gas motor cannot spark and ignite the gas which is not there, however hot the ignition points may be, so the heart and mind cannot develop spiritual power when the knowledge of how to do so is absent. The reading of good books should be part of every sincere Christian person's program. Money should be spared for this, even at the cost of allowing some other things to go. Wherever reading and interest in gathering knowledge are found there exist a wide-awake, appreciative, growing mind and heart; in their absence there is leanness, and often stumbling in the Christian's life. The mind must be fed as well as the body if it is to develop into a healthy, enlightened Christian mind.

When the children of Israel complained in the wilderness about not having meat and spoke scornfully about the "manna" God had given them, God gave them quails in abundance but sent "leanness into their soul." This is a practical illustration of what happens when God's people become dissatisfied with His way and will for them and begin to seek outside interests for satisfaction. It matters not what the diversion sought nor how harmless it may appear outwardly, if this is allowed to take the place and time needed for soul culture and development, it will bring leanness to the soul. No amount of reasoning nor argument about its harmlessness—not even to note that others who are spiritual participate—will change its effect upon one who allows any such thing to come between him and his soul's developmental program. "Whether therefore ye eat, or drink, or whatsoever ye do, do all to the glory of God" (I Cor. 10:31) should become the governing rule of the life of the Spirit-filled believer. When this becomes his rule of life and Christ is put where He rightfully belongs, he will find that he can enjoy all things which God has given rightly to be enjoyed without a pang of conscience for having neglected the *first things first* rule of spiritual life.

CHAPTER XXI

Danger of Getting into Ruts

Mention should be made of this danger in passing. Someone has aptly said that a "rut is a grave with both ends knocked out." There are ruts in all of life into which people almost inadvertently fall but which none the less have their deadening effect upon them. The mind and the nerve reflexes play tricks on the best of us if we are not careful. One of man's best allies is the fact that he can establish patterns of behavior which become reflex actions and greatly aid him in his daily tasks, such as putting on his clothes, driving a car, and many other things. Yet this same fixedness can prove fatal to his growth if it is not governed. Because a thing has been done a certain way for ten years does not mean that it may not be done in a better way. It is the fellow who can see the better way of doing things and is adaptable to change who gets ahead and makes the necessary progress in life to keep civilization moving forward.

It would seem that the people who are led by the Spirit and who "walk in the Spirit" should be the last people to become lost in ruts in life.

Sometimes one develops a rut in his reading habits, or in his prayer habits, or in the way of conducting family worship. Too many of us are given to "vain repetitions" in our worship and have too little variety. Are there not many new things for which to thank God daily, many new requests and many situations of change which need our attention?

Many people are so "situated" in the same pew at church that they become greatly disturbed if they are asked to move for some occasion. They have sat there and allowed latecomers to "climb over their knees" for so long that to show the courtesy of sitting at the other end of the pew would be a tremendous shock to their emotional nature!

Ruts are often firmly established by church leaders in the form of service. The New Testament is the most informal of all books about worship. No method is anywhere prescribed and no form set up to follow. Certainly, some form is a necessity in ordinary worship services, but could not Spirit-filled people have also a bit more variety in their services? Should there even be a service so strictly held to form that there is no place in it for the witness for Christ when someone in the congregation feels within him a welling up testimony of praise? Much indeed is lost when this formal order of things crowds out the more free expressions of praises to God. The Spirit is often grieved by the coldness of our form and the lack of spiritual discernment on the part of both leaders and laymen. We should strive to avoid the pitfalls of ruts in our lives, both privately and in public worship.

Chapter XXII

Danger of False Impressions

Just as there is danger of getting into ruts which sidetrack us, so there is the need to be ever watchful lest false impressions lead us astray on the other hand. For a definition of impressions from above and below and how to judge them we present a quotation from Knapp. Concerning false impressions he says:

> 1. They are inward impressions made upon our spirits. 2. They are often very strong impressions. Fanaticism is born in the land of strong but wrong impressions. 3. They occur repeatedly. See how Satan persisted with our first parents, Job and Jesus. . . . 4. They frequently occur during prayer and other devotions. Nothing is more in keeping with their object than to divert from communion with God. . . . 5. Like good impressions they may be brought to us by our friends. Job had more trouble from his friends than from affliction and Satan combined. . . . 6. Wrong impressions may be attended by a chain of circumstances which seem to confirm their truthfulness. Satan is allowed great latitude, and shows great cunning in arranging his program to thwart divine purposes. . . . 7. Wrong impressions may be, and often, though not always are, in harmony with our natural desires . . . 8. Evil impressions may also, like the good, be attended by striking passages of Scripture, which seem to sanction them . . . Like those from above, they may come suddenly and unexpectedly.[9]

There is only one sure way to test an impression such as these and that is by the Word of God and earnest prayer. It is almost certain that any impression accompanied by a spirit of hurry and haste is not of God. When there is with the impression a sense of "if you do not do this at once, you will sin against God," one had better check it again before venturing. That oft-quoted passage about "the king's business requires haste" is no divine directive to anyone (I Sam. 21:8), and was not necessarily all the truth. But there is a divine directive that is true and will pay to be heeded in such matters as this, "He that is hasty of spirit exalteth folly" (Prov. 14:29).

One may also test an impression by whether it stacks up with what is positively right morally, ethically, and spiritually. If it is out of line in any of these points it cannot be of God, however strong it may be. Sometimes impressions appear to meet all these tests but are not in keeping with common sense. If this type of impression persists, however, so that the person becomes in bondage to having to stop people indiscriminately and constantly to speak to them, it is likely a false impression and the person is doing little or no good by heeding it; perhaps, even harm is coming from it. Most spiritually minded persons have, at some time or another, had Satan fool them by heeding some sudden impression, as was the case with the author when a mere boy. The impression to stop before a large house where the living room lights were brightly burning and a car was parked in front became so strong one night that it would hardly be passed up. It carried with it the implication that the young fellow whose car was parked there was on a date and would soon be out. Since no one had probably even spoken to him about his soul and he might be eternally lost if this opportunity to help him were passed up, moral obligation demanded that he must be spoken to that night. After waiting in the cold for a long time and no one ever coming out, I finally had to abandon the project, and with a sad but wiser heart completed the homeward trek.

Not a few people by allowing mistaken impressions to lead them have gotten themselves into embarrassing situations. Many years ago in the southland there lived a very godly lady who was taken into such a situation by Satan. The impression was made upon her mind that she must go to a sister whose little girl was allowed to wear clothes like a boy, which to this sister was a very grave mistake. After considerable prayer for courage she went and had a talk with the sister about her girl's manner of dress. The mother asked, "Are you sure the Lord sent you to talk to me about this?" When the lady assured her she was, the mother proceded to explain that the little "girl" was a boy whose hair they had just postponed to cut because it was so pretty!

Many cases of far worse consequences could be cited of people who have allowed mistaken impressions to lead them astray, some indeed into deep sin, as a result of following the wrong lead at first.

When impressions are of God, He will see to it that they are made so plain that one cannot be well deceived by them. If one misses the opportunity to carry out the impression, if it is of God, and the person is sincere, God will give him another opportunity to get it done. It is better to verify the fact that it is God's will and be safe than to jump to hasty conclusions and have lasting regrets or hinder the work of God by so doing. Often Satan will sidetrack one ever so little just to get him started in the wrong direction. This must be zealously guarded against.

CHAPTER XXIII

Danger from Worry

Is "worry" consistent with the experience of heart purity? Can one who is filled with the Spirit even worry without grieving the Spirit? Much depends upon what is meant by worry, for there are many different opinions about what constitutes worry and not all of them would be found in any dictionary. For example, some think of worry as any form of anxious care; others say they were worried when in reality they were angry.

Baldwin has a good definition of what he calls carnal worry:

> That spirit of chafing at divine providence which causes me to doubt God, or inwardly complain at His dealings with me, is carnal; that spirit which meets the rebuffs and insults of sinners, or, it may be the slights and misunderstandings of my brethren, with a complaining and resentful heart is carnal; that spirit which meets circumstances with grumbling, or which becomes carnally fretful and peevish under physical disability, is carnal; and that spirit which meets the temptations of the devil with an inward complaint which involves the integrity and versatility of the Almighty is carnal. Thus we see that carnal worry involves my integrity as a holy man; it disconnects me from God by my doubtfulness and complaints.[10]

This type of worry is what may be better defined as a spirit of peevish fretfulness arising out of an unholy disposition which tends to blame God for the unhappy circumstances of life and is not content to trust Him for their outcome. Even in the midst of life's hardest trial Job "sinned not, nor charged God foolishly" (Job 1:22). Under severe testings one may feel the pressure of the devil, tempting him to complain about his circumstances, and yet in heart not yield to it. It is the inward condition of the soul which may determine the spirit manifested.

But to maintain that if one is filled with the Spirit he will have always a cheerful outlook upon life and never be conscious of a care is going farther than St. Paul went.

In what ways may one be said to worry without that worry arising from a carnal heart? The answer to this, again, may vary with different individuals, for not all persons are constituted alike. But generally speaking it may be said that one may have an anxious mind about his children, work, financial conditions, or other such matters and yet not have carnal worry in his heart. It is true that Wesley made "anxious care" appear to be outside the sphere of perfect love, but it is doubtful if the Apostle Paul did.

So long as we dwell in broken physical bodies, subject to all the nervous reactions which beset many, it will be impossible to get entirely away from times when the mind will be troubled and perplexed about many things. As Baldwin has pointed out, "Worry, or the disposition thereto, is in some sense a constitutional disorder. In such a case it is no more a sure sign of carnal conditions than is dyspepsia or liver complaint.[11]

St. Paul spoke of being perplexed and troubled on every hand. Jesus was grieved because of the hardness of people's hearts. There is a sense in which a holy man may chafe under the restraints which keep him from being at his best for the Lord, or in seeing Christ's cause misrepresented by someone, or seeing another manifest a spirit of bigotry.

One may be deeply anxious for the welfare of a loved one or troubled because of the delay of a message from a dear one and yet not be carnal in so doing. The absence of sufficient funds to feed and clothe the family may keep a holy man awake at night, restless, not knowing which way to turn. This may arise from his nervous condition rather than from lack of faith in God. It is easy to condemn the other person for such apparent lack of faith until one experiences such a state himself.

There are times when the actions of others may vex or annoy one, or when circumstances beyond his control may give him restless moments. Some people are so happily constituted that they seem never to be perturbed by their surroundings. They can be calm in almost any circumstance. But not everyone is so constituted mentally and emotionally. What appears to some as fretfulness on the part of another may be only nervous restlessness, the result of excitability or instability of disposition. It is entirely possible to have a troubled mind to the extent that the brow furrows, the nerves twitch, and the body feels a sense of uneasiness and yet to have a perfect calm deep within the soul, so far as faith in God and the repose of the soul upon Christ are concerned.

From all this it may be concluded that the forms of manifestations of worry listed above may be consistent with a pure heart, but that there are dangers against which every saint must guard. What is only natural worry may be allowed to develop into a peevish fretfulness of spirit which will rob one of his faith in God and open the door to carnal anxiety, born of unbelief. There is a fine prescription for curing worry in Psalms 37:1-8. If one will read and accept this for his daily guide in facing the trying circumstances of life, it will go far toward curing all anxious fears which may be harmful to him.

CHAPTER XXIV

Faith and Works

Perhaps a brief note of warning should here be sounded concerning the dangers which may arise from either extreme of faith and works. It will be remembered that Paul was the great apostle of faith while James emphasized the necessity of good works. Some have felt that Paul and James could not be reconciled in their two extreme positions but this is not the case. Paul deals with that "faith without works," which is "dead." Faith, for Paul, then, is that utter dependence upon Christ alone for salvation; while "works," for James, do not amount to salvation, but are the fruits of a righteousness which one cannot possess without them.

The dangers here may be simply stated in this way: We must ever be on guard against depending too much upon God and doing too little in co-operation with Him to produce the results of a truly well-rounded Christian life. This is the danger of those who push faith to its extreme. Good works for them do not count. They seldom speak to anyone about Christ, often are slow to witness for Him, and feel that one needs only to keep in personal touch with God. This leads to the danger of losing this gracious experience by failure to "let your light so shine before men, that they may see your good works, and glorify your Father which is in heaven" (Matt. 5:16). This is part of everyone's duty as a believer, and one may not shun it except at the peril of his experience with Christ. This is not referring to a "show of good works," or religion on the coat sleeve; far from it. It is rather that particular allowing of one's life and testimony to shine forth without being hindered, that Christ may thereby be glorified.

On the other hand there is the ever-present danger of those who would depend too much upon their own works and too little upon the Holy Spirit. They tend to take things into their own hands, make out their program as they see best, and then hope for God to bless it. This class may be illustrated by the minister who said that before he was sanctified he used to go through his library and develop his sermon during the week for Sunday, then search through the Bible on Saturday for a text that would fit his sermon. Plainly, he was depending upon himself and asking God to accommodate himself to his program. There is much more danger in this kind of thinking than is sometimes seen. It is possible to trust human ingenuity to scheme out the plans even in God's work and then expect Him to bless the plans without realizing as one might that he is doing this very thing. God expects us to use the talent He has given us, it is true, but He also expects us to await divine directions where this is so essential to the success of His works.

Chapter XXV

Danger of Spiritual Drought

Too often when people are consciously clear that they have been filled with the Spirit and are wholly the Lord's they are inclined to take the attitude that *this is it,* and it is not necessary to bother further about special refreshings. So long as one prays regularly and keeps his soul in harmony with God he will not necessarily need extra refreshings. His experience will run on something like perpetual motion. This is too often the unconscious philosophy upon which many operate.

It is true that there should always be grace sufficient in the heart of a Spirit-filled believer for every emergency of life and that he may at all times so live by the grace of God. This is not only possible but desirable in normal Christian experience. But it is not always the case, unfortunately, with many. No one can say that a person who may not have an emotional overflow of blessing every day is living behind light or beneath his privileges, for not everyone is so constituted as to have so even an emotional pattern. One can keep the approbation of God upon his life, however, at all times and will if he is obedient to the Spirit. But despite all this there are many times in one's life when he sorely needs a "refreshing . . . from the presence of the Lord." The accumulations of the passing days of care and trial may so fill one's eyes with earthly dust that he needs them washed with the tears of an unusual overflow of divine grace. There are always times in every person's life when he needs to get quiet before God and search his heart and wait for God's whisperings to his soul. In the hurry and bustle of the day one may find himself off course if he does not keep a keen ear for the gentle whisperings of the Spirit of God.

No great revival has ever broken out without some of God's saints first having paid the price for a refreshing upon their own souls. When the church prevails with God for this reassuring baptism of blessing, she can expect an awakening of the unsaved about her, but not before. When the disciples returned from the persecution which followed the healing of the lame man and had a mighty prayer meeting, they were met with such a time of refreshing from on high that the place where they had assembled was "shaken." It was after this that they went out again with great boldness to preach the Word and many more were "added unto the Lord" (Acts 4). Each one personally needs refreshings from God all along. Sometimes when under trial one needs this refreshing for reassurance; sometimes when becoming lean in spirit he needs it for drawing him closer to God; sometimes when in great "heaviness through manifold temptations" he needs it to give strength and power to be faithful unto the end; and always one needs it for the power to witness for Christ.

CHAPTER XXVI

Danger of
Seeking a Human Holiness

The world about us is full of human religion. Christianity has been cursed and blighted more from this than any other one evil within the Church. There are now whole segments of Christianity, historically so called, which are honeycombed with this thing. Confessionals, priests, high altars, self-denials, and many forms of works are accepted as the means by which millions expect to see God at the end of life's journey. How sad that countless millions will awake eternally shocked at their fate! Within Protestantism are more millions who depend far too largely upon sacraments and good works for their eternal salvation.

The ranks of the Spirit-filled group of believers has not escaped certain influences of this vast movement which through the centuries has placed far too much stress upon human works. One must be always upon his guard not to allow Satan to push him into a seeking after holiness by works, such as fasting, bodily abuses, self-denials, and the like. And here is the keen line of danger, in that there are times when these things are essential to growth and development spiritually and one will find that to ignore them brings leanness of soul. But there is also the ever-present danger that one will allow such things as these to become a part of his spiritual program, substituting them for signs of real spirituality. This was the Pharisees' religion, you recall, and it was obnoxious to Christ. Fastings, self-denials, going the second mile with someone, and many other things are by-products of deep spiritual living, and are also helpful means to promoting this life. But they must never become the chief ends in one's life of holiness. Separateness from worldliness, while commendable and essential in its proper place in Christian living, can, nevertheless, become a kind of badge of spirituality which one depends upon as the evidence of his Christlikeness. So may these other things. *Our* holiness is obnoxious to God; it savors of self-righteousness and pride, and He cannot approve of it. We cannot trust in it for security in Christ for even a moment. There is no "true holiness" but that which flows from Christ and which we take from Him moment by moment. We are in danger every moment that we trust our own good works of piety or charity, for we are then not fully trusting Christ. Let it be plain that these good works do accompany full salvation and without them one will hardly be able to survive spiritually, but the danger is that one should ever rely upon them for salvation, for even a moment.

On the other hand there are those whose supreme error has been the rejection of all such means of grace as having no part in salvation nor accompanying it. Their repudiation of the works of the Church has been too harsh and they are in danger of going to the extreme which accepts Christ as the sole means of salvation, denying that even any good works accompany grace in the heart. They claim that Christ's righteousness is imputed to those who believe, and even though they may continue in sin, they will be saved through His merits, without any work of righteousness. There is a serious danger in this belief, for one may be deceived into accepting a so-called "positional relationship" to Christ, without having the actual saving relationship, and thus in the end be lost.

CHAPTER XXVII

Danger of Inordinate Affection

So long as we are in the flesh there will need to be proper guards set up against any form of human relationships which may prove harmful to our spiritual welfare. When Christians are faced with difficult home situations, especially where one of the companions is not favorable to the religious life of the other, or for some other reason not fully compatible, they must be ever on the alert lest what at first is only mutual Christian fellowship may be allowed to bloom into something detrimental to themselves and others. The affections naturally are attracted to any mutual emotional current. This in itself is harmless but it must always be held in check, that there may never develop an attraction which is out of ethical or moral bounds. Sometimes a grave danger exists where one feels that he is emotionally cheated by his companion of that care and devotion which is normally craved by everyone, and another person is especially thoughtful of his wishes or welfare. There may at first be nothing more than the mere desire to be sociable on the part of one or both parties, but if not guarded it will grow into something more. Spiritual affinities develop between persons of "kindred minds" along spiritual lines, or sometimes between those who have had similar experiences of hardship or trial. The very fact that the fellowship of Christian faith provides within it a warmth and mutual interest in all those who are within its scope makes this danger even more imminent.

Nor does it stop with persons of the opposite sex, but inordinate affection in another form may develop even in families or among friends of the same sex. It is not always with a view to sensuality that this type of affection develops. Anderson has a fine caution upon this point:

> The love which enslaves the reason and will is not pure; it is inordinate. This may be a love for persons who have no spiritual life as well as for those who do. It may be love for those who are related by the ties of blood and family. And it may be a love for those who are related in other ways. The favor, friendship and reciprocated love of these may be greatly desired, which is natural that it should be. But so to love them as to heed their advice, which, if obeyed, would lead to acts that would displease God and impoverish the soul, is inordinate affection. The love which Adam had for his wife he let exceed the bounds of his reason and will. He took of the fruit and did eat. It led to his wilful sin. Many sanctified persons have been enticed from the way of holiness because they have compromised through their natural human affections. They loved unwisely. There is nothing sinful in the human affections. But they must never go beyond the proper bounds which God has placed about them.[12]

When one sees his affections for another developing to the point where his loyalty to God along any line is called into question, he must stop and take his affections into check at once. Not even as companions can persons allow their love for each other to come between them and God's will for them. As long as the heart is the abode of the Holy Spirit, He will always check one when he is in danger. But the nature of affection is such that one must guard it carefully or it will so blind and deafen one that he will have difficulty recognizing the checks of the Spirit, or else turn to false reasoning that there can be no harm in this particular thing.

Ministers and church people in places to advise others must be particularly cautious when counseling persons of the opposite sex, especially with reference to any marital difficulties. One is often on dangerous ground when doing so. Sometimes his sympathies may go out to the troubled person and he is thereby brought to a place where extreme caution should be taken, especially when the person seeking aid comes more than once for consultation. Satan attacks through pure love or true sympathy at first but may gradually lead the individuals into a closer mutual fellowship until there arises between them an affinity which will lead them to the brink of sin. One must always heed the checks of the Spirit and use common sense in such relationships or he will inevitably come to sorrow.

Young people must likewise be on guard against the development of inordinate affection both between the opposite sexes and between those of the same sex. With youthful, untested emotions which grasp for fulfillment, often infatuation is taken at first for love and sometimes considerable damage is done before those involved are aware of what is happening. The difference between infatuation and love is that the former desires immediate gratification in extreme petting and such things, whereas the latter is more deeply interested in the personal welfare and happiness of the object of affection. It will not require long to examine the motives and affections and discover the differences.

Chapter XXVIII

Danger of Casting Away Confidence

The Bible warns us, "Cast not away therefore your confidence, which hath great recompense of reward. For ye have need of patience, that after ye have done the will of God, ye might receive the promise" (Heb. 10: 35-36). It is one of the supreme tricks of Satan to persuade persons to cast away their confidence in times of deep depression or when for some reason they have been trapped into something which in the light of the Spirit's chastising they see was wrong. There are other times, when friends fail or foes persecute and one becomes temporarily discouraged, that Satan suggests that one might as well quit. It is his aim to rob God of the honor of the faith of all the people he can; therefore to get one to cast away his confidence is a great victory for him.

Many times when one is in the midst of heaviness and dark trial the archfiend of deception will come to whisper doubts and questionings into the mind. This is especially true of younger Christians and of those who have not been long in the way of full salvation. If Satan can instill doubts he has gone far toward defeating one. Anderson has written an encouraging word of warning to such persons:

> Illness of body and mind can produce times of depression in spirit. Under such trials one can easily exaggerate his own faults and failures. This leads to self-condemnation and self-depreciation. One may believe in such times that the Lord is about to give him up because he has been so unfaithful and impatient under trial. He may even be driven to extreme fear that the unpardonable sin has been committed.[13]

It is no evidence that one has lost the victory because he is under pressure from Satan and circumstances. He should hold steady and refuse to allow Satan to persuade him to lose heart or confidence. Sometimes one must take his liberty in the Lord at such times and refuse to be governed in his devotions by how he feels. Brengle has given some excellent advice upon this subject:

> Many a soul, in fierce temptation and hellish [gloom] has poured out his heart in prayer and then sunk back in despair, who, if he had only closed his prayer with thanks, and dared in the name of God to shout, would have filled hell with confusion, and won a victory that would have struck all the harps of heaven and made the angels shout with glee.[14]

Sometimes the difference between victory and defeat is a person's determination to take God by faith and declare his purpose anew and proclaim it to the devil.

Satan often tempts one to throw away his confidence because of imperfections of service or shortcomings in his life in some way. One is sometimes tempted to feel that his service to Christ is of such poor nature that he is not acceptable. Watson has an excellent passage upon this point:

> You must remember that the principle of obedience is one thing—that lies in the heart—but the application of that principle is something else. There is no suffering in the principles of obedience. The element of loyalty lies in heart, and there is no suffering in that. But when you take that principle of loyalty, of obedience in the heart, and come to apply it to the outward life, it necessarily involves a great deal of suffering. And Jesus learned how to apply the principle of obedience by the things which He suffered.[15]

Just so it may be with the follower of Christ. His heart may feel at all times the throb of a perfect obedience to God but he may not always find the avenue of perfect service. And when he fails there will always be the sense of unworthiness which possesses him, even though he tried his reasonable best. We are not like the Saviour in that respect, for He had a human perfection of knowledge and other advantages which we do not possess. God will never hold one responsible beyond his capacity to perform; of this we may rest assured. As Anderson has well said, "Sanctification does not call for services to be performed beyond what one can reasonably do. It calls for a pure life, but not an unequal task."[16]

A rule or so for service to Christ may here be submitted. Fletcher warned that if one wished to live the most beneficial life of the Spirit he should watch against certain things: "Beware of suffering your affections to be entangled by worldly vanities, your imagination to amuse itself with unprofitable objects, and of indulging yourself in the commission of what are called small faults."[17] Such indulgences naturally provide the means of the leakage of spiritual power from the life.

Never allow any present trial to eclipse the fact that there will be a brighter day. It could be the very trial through which one passes holds the seeds which will be the harbingers of a brighter day. Well did Bishop Taylor say:

> Yes, the saint may weep under the crushing burden of his cross, but the Sun of Righteousness shining through the prism of his tears will throw the supernal rainbow of peace across his darkest sky. The saint may sigh with sorrow over his losses, but as Pan in the Greek fable sighed over the apparently worthless reeds which were left in his hands when the object of his affection eluded his grasp, and was surprised to hear the reeds waken into music as his sighs breathed through them, so the sighs of the saints are quickly transformed into song.[18]

One cannot too often look back to past experiences where defeat has been suffered without dampening his spirit but, like the great Apostle Paul in this respect, he can make it his rule to do as he did: "Forgetting those things which are behind, . . . I press toward the mark for the prize of the high calling of God in Christ Jesus" (Phil. 3:13).

Another good rule is to accept yourself as yourself and stop berating yourself for not being better or more successful. Hadfield makes a reference to James, the eminent psychologist, who told of a lady who said that the happiest day of her life was the day she *ceased trying to be beautiful.* He adds this very helpful comment:

> The strain after the impossible is so great that thousands break down over it. So few of us are content to be ourselves, yet by seeking to be another we end by failing to be either. *No man can ever be other than himself,* and the attempt to be what we can never be is a hopeless misadventure, resulting in the loss of individuality.[19]

It is hardly necessary to remark that, while it is excellent to note the virtues of friends and especially more earnest Chirstians and accept good patterns of behavior and spiritual progress from them, it is folly to try to fully emulate them. One only succeeds in failure and self-condemnation when he does.

Perhaps a word about restoration in case of the loss of spiritual ground would be in place in taking leave of this subject. When one has lost out and is seeking restoration, there are pitfalls which must be guarded against. Anderson has put the case in point well:

> Many people fail at this point, by constantly looking for the same emotions and joy they had when they were first saved, and they refuse to believe because they do not have the same old experience. Do you remember that the children of Israel went into captivity several times after they had entered Canaan? But never did God divide Jordan for them again. God never took them in again

in the same manner as at first . . . It is not a blessing
you want, but the Blesser, Whom you have shut out by
your unbelief.[20]

In this connection we shall only mention briefly the
old question of whether or not a restoration may be made
all the way from a backslidden condition to full sanctification at once. To some this may be a new idea but
not to those acquainted with the position of Wesley and
others. Smith, who quotes Wesley at large, is of the
opinion that when a backslider comes to God for restoration he must necessarily be restored from as much light
and grace as he fell from. The logic of the opinion is
based upon the fact that God could not restore a person
while walking in less than all the light he once had, and
that if one who was once fully sanctified comes to God
for restoration he must of necessity obey that full light.
In this light, if he walks in all the light he once knew,
"the blood of Jesus Christ his Son cleanseth" him from
all sin.[21] It would be difficult, however, for the average
backslider to so grasp this truth theologically as to come
back to God as fully and completely as the theory states,
in many instances. His preconceived opinion of the necessity of two applications of redemption's provision in regeneration and sanctification, as at the beginning, would
likely hinder his faith from taking in the whole step of
restoration. However, it is a matter upon which the
individual must be satisfied when he is restored. We
have witnessed cases where a person was restored to
saving grace and also to full salvation before leaving the
place of prayer.

It should be pointed out here that in cases where
the person has grieved the Spirit to the extent that he
feels he must ask forgiveness of God for the act which
led to this condition, but has not broken with God by a
prolonged attitude of disobedience, the restoration is
complete the instant of forgiveness. He has not in reality
backslidden in the common acceptation of the term and

should not allow Satan to destroy his confidence in the restoring love and favor of God. To seek again to be both saved and filled with the Spirit every time a minor offense or infraction against the Spirit has been committed is to so cast away confidence as to destroy it.

It may be illustrated in this way. We may often offend a friend to the extent of saying, "I am sorry; forgive me for my thoughtlessness." But we would hardly go through all the procedures of a case where a serious offense had been committed and friendship completely broken. Is it not reasonable to suppose that our Heavenly Father is as understanding as our friends?

Chapter XXIX

Danger of
Grieving the Spirit

It is doubtful if there are any Christians who never in their lives from the day of their baptism with the Spirit until death so live as never to grieve the Holy Spirit in some sense. There are degrees of grieving, withstanding, and resisting the Spirit. To these last two extremes the Spirit-filled believer does not go, for he respects that injunction of Paul, "And grieve not the holy Spirit . . . whereby ye are sealed unto the day of redemption" (Eph. 4:30). We may grieve the Spirit by our getting ahead of Him in our attempts to do service for God, or by our slowness in response to His leadings. Sometimes by too much talking and particularly when it is of a jesting nature, we may grieve Him. Any act which does not harmonize with God's highest design for our lives is in some sense a grief to the Spirit. Young people often grieve Him by their lax social actions, carrying petting and the like to extremes which bring condemnation to them and cause them to feel the need of forgiveness. Older people may also grieve Him by overindulgences of various kinds by which they are weakened and hindered in their service for the Master.

These are the somewhat daily infractions against the Spirit of grace, some of which may be done half-consciously, due to our human infirmities. While they are by no means pleasing to God and must have the atonement moment by moment, they do not constitute such breaches of the covenant of grace as to leave one entirely out of grace and backslidden. Some things mentioned above bring one to the brink of the loss of grace, and if one does not fly to the Blood with a heart-felt cry for pardon, he will soon find himself under condemnation which has guilt attached to it. Perhaps it should be said here that what one sometimes feels under such circumstances as the beginning of condemnation is in reality the "chastening of the Lord," for surely the Lord will chasten everyone before cutting him off from His grace. If one comes immediately to God to care for the thing which has grieved the Spirit, he may be restored to full fellowship without a breach in his covenant relationship sufficient to be called a "break with God." Many sincere souls could not truly say they had willfully turned away from God, but they witness keen inward disapproval of the Spirit. This is God's chastising, drawing and warning them that they must repair the matter before a breach is made.

The grieving of the Spirit which amounts to a breaking with God is that form of continued withstanding of His pleadings to rectify our wrong act or attitude which has brought about the grief to begin with. This will eventually develop into a "resisting" of the Spirit. At just what juncture the Spirit may take His departure from a person thus grieving Him none can tell, for no two persons have the same degree of light or ability to respond to chastisement and the like. Therefore, the Spirit alone can determine when one has gone to that extent where He must of necessity depart from him and so cut off his fellowship with God. But this much is certain: God will do all He can to bring the person to the terms of His covenant and to effect a reconciliation before His Spirit departs from him. Sometimes this work of the Spirit precedes the act of sin, as when the individual is premeditating some wrong act, and the Spirit must depart when the decision has been finally made to sin in spite of His pleadings. But more often the individual of a spiritual life commits the offense quickly or thoughtlessly and must be dealt with afterward. But we may rest assured that God, "who is rich in mercy," will always see that everything possible is done to secure the person against losing his grace from the heart.

Everyone should be always on guard against grieving the Spirit. If one lives so as not to grieve the Spirit he may be sure of constant victory, whatever his emotional ups and downs may be.

It is the author's sincere prayer that the message of this book may aid many to solve the problems they have met in living the Spirit-filled life. If this is the case, his prayers will be answered.

Notes

SECTION ONE

1. Dean Stanley, *Christian Institutions*, p. 251. (Quoted from *The Holy Spirit*, by J. A. Huffman, p. 27.)
2. J. A. Huffman, *The Holy Spirit*, p. 119.
3. P. B. Fitzwater, *Christian Theology*, p. 185.
4. Henry C. Thiessen, *Lectures in Systematic Theology*, p. 144.
5. Huffman, *op. cit.*, pp. 27-28.
6. *Ibid.*, pp. 40-43.
7. *Ibid.*, p. 43.
8. *Ibid.*, p. 172.
9. *Encyclopaedia Britannica*, Vol. XI, "The Holy Spirit."
10. *Ibid. in loco.*
11. John 3:5.
12. Biederwolf, *Helps to the Study of the Holy Spirit;* R. A. Torrey, *Baptism with the Holy Spirit;* R. Cumming, *Through the Eternal Spirit.*
13. Amos Binney and Daniel Steele, *Binney's Theological Compend*, "Sanctification."
14. John Wesley, *Plain Account of Christian Perfection*, pp. 1-2.
15. *Ibid.*, p. 14.
16. *Ibid.*, p. 24.
17. J. T. Peck, *The Central Idea of Christianity*, p. 193.
18. S. L. Brengle, *Helps to Holiness*, p. 8.
19. Binney and Steele, *op. cit.*
20. *Harper's Analytical Greek Lexicon.*
21. Biederwolf, *op. cit.*, "Comforter."
22. Wesley, *op. cit.*, pp. 1-30.
23. See Note 12, p. 33, of this section. Billy Graham, *Revival in Our Time*, "Baptism with the Holy Spirit."

SECTION TWO

1. Wesley, *op. cit.*, pp. 9 ff.
2. Forman Lincicome, *Three D's of the Sanctified*, p. 43.
3. S. A. Keen, *Pentecostal Papers*, p. 81.
4. H. A. Baldwin, *Holiness and the Human Element*, p. 75.
5. *Ibid.*, pp. 89-90.
6. *Ibid.*, p. 90.
7. J. G. Lawson, *Deeper Experiences of Famous Christians*, pp. 199-200.
8. Carney Landis and M. M. Bolles, *Abnormal Psychology*, p. 301.
9. *Ibid.*, p. 292.
10. Lincicome, *op. cit.*, p. 39.
11. Wesley, *op. cit.*, p. 47.
12. Peter Wiseman, *Biblical Perfection*, pp. 18-19.
13. Lincicome, *op. cit.*, p. 32.

SECTION THREE

1. Binney and Steele, *op. cit.*, p. 132.
2. Lawson, *op. cit.*, pp. 87-134.
3. Rene Pache, *The Person and Work of the Holy Spirit*, p. 169.

4. R. S. Taylor, *A Right Conception of Sin*, p. 63.

5. Lincicome, *op. cit.*, pp. 45-46.

6. Wesley, *op. cit.*, p. 15.

7. Baldwin, *op. cit.*, pp. 81-82.

8. *Harper's Analytical Greek Lexicon*.

9. J. A. Hadfield, *Psychology and Morals*, p. 169.

10. Mary A. Tenney, *Blueprint for a Christian World*, p. 189.

11. Adam Clarke, *Commentary*, VI, 290.

12. Lincicome, *op. cit.*, pp. 59-60.

13. Baldwin, *op. cit.*, pp. 48 ff.

14. Charles G. Finney, *Lectures to Professing Christians*, p. 340.

15. Wm. S. Deal, *The Furnace of Affliction*, p. 36.

16. John Wesley, *Sermons*, I, 458, 460.

17. B. Carradine, *Pastoral Sketches*.

18. Wm. S. Deal, *Problems of Modern Youth*.

19. Lincicome, *op. cit.*, pp. 48-49.

20. Wesley, *Sermons, op. cit.*, pp. 466-67.

21. Hester Ann Rogers, *Life and Journal*, p. 124.

22. Baldwin, *op. cit.*, p. 17.

23. Wesley, *Plain Account of Christian Perfection, op. cit.*, p. 37.

24. Landis and Bolles, *op. cit.*

25. Wesley, *Sermons, op. cit.*, pp. 113 ff.

26. M. G. Pearse, *The Christianity of Jesus Christ*, p. 179.

27. Baldwin, *op. cit., pp.* 60-61.

28. J. Stafford Wright, *Man in the Process of Time*, p. 36.

29. Wesley, *Plain Account of Christian Perfection, op. cit.*, p. 20.

SECTION FOUR

1. H. E. Jessop, *Foundations of Doctrine*, pp. 135-36.

2. Joseph Benson, *The Life of Rev. John Fletcher*, p. 80.

3. Baldwin, *op. cit.*, p. 17.

4. Wesley, *Plain Account of Chrisitan Perfection, op. cit.*, p. 38.

5. Brengle, *op. cit.*, p. 109.

6. Jessop, *op. cit.*, pp. 117-18 (Cook, *New Testament Holiness*).

7. Henry E. Brockett, *Scriptural Freedom from Sin*, p. 167.

8. T. M. Anderson, *After Sanctification*, p. 30.

9. M. W. Knapp, *Impressions from Above and Below*, pp. 20-21.

10. Baldwin, *op. cit.*, p. 125.

11. *Ibid.*, p. 67.

12. Anderson, *op. cit.*, p. 57.

13. *Ibid.*, p. 67.

14. Brengle, *op. cit.*, p. 125.

15. G. D. Watson, *Love Abounding*, p. 202.

16. Anderson, *op. cit.*, p. 32.

17. Benson, *op. cit.*, p. 87.

18. J. Paul Taylor, *The Music of Pentecost*, p. 102.

19. Hadfield, *op. cit.*, pp. 212-13.

20. Anderson, *op. cit.*, p. 74.

21. See Wm. M. Smith, *The Backslider's Return*, for full discussion of this theory.

Bibliography

ANDERSON, T. M. *After Sanctification.* Kansas City: Beacon Hill Press, 1951.

BALDWIN, H. A. *Holiness and the Human Element.* (3rd ed.). Kansas City: Beacon Hill Press, 1953.

BENSON, JOSEPH. *Life of Rev. John Fletcher.* New York: Eaton and Mains, undated.

BIEDERWOLF, WILLIAM. *Helps to the Study of the Holy Spirit.* Grand Rapids: Zondervan Publishing House, 1903.

BINNEY, AMOS, and STEELE, DANIEL. *Binney's Theological Compend.* Nashville: Abingdon-Cokesbury Press, 1902.

BRENGLE, S. L. *Helps to Holiness.* London: Salvationist Publishing and Supplies, 1927.

BROCKETT, HENRY E. *Scriptural Freedom from Sin.* Kansas City: Beacon Hill Press, 1941.

CARRADINE, B. *Pastoral Sketches.* Louisville: Pentecostal Publishing Co.

CLARKE, ADAM. *Commentary,* Vol. VI. Nashville: Abingdon-Cokesbury Press, undated.

CUMMING, R. *Through the Eternal Spirit.* Chicago: Moody Press.

DEAL, WM. S. *The Furnace of Affliction.* Apollo: West Publishing Co., 1948.

DEAL, WM. S. and MYRNA A. *Problems of Modern Youth.* Apollo: West Publishing Co., 1952.

Encyclopaedia Britannica. Chicago: Encyclopaedia Britannica, Inc., 1953.

FINNEY, CHAS. G. *Lectures to Professing Christians.* New York: Fleming H. Revell, 1897.

FITZWATER, P. B. *Christian Theology.* Grand Rapids: Wm. B. Eerdmans, 1938.

GRAHAM, BILLY. *Revival in Our Time.* Wheaton: Van Kampen Press, 1950.

Harper's Analytical Greek Lexicon. New York: Harper and Sons, undated.

HADFIELD, J. A. *Psychology and Morals.* London: Methuen & Co. Ltd., 1949.

HUFFMAN, J. A. *The Holy Spirit.* Winona Lake: Standard Press, 1938.

JESSOP, H. E. *Foundations of Doctrine.* Winona Lake: Free Methodist Publishing House, 1938.

KEEN, S. A. *Pentecostal Papers.* Apollo: West Publishing Co., 1946.

KNAPP, M. W. *Impressions from Above and Below.* Cincinnati: Revivalist Press, 1892.

LANDIS, CARNEY, and BOLLES, M. M. *Abnormal Psychology.* New York: Macmillan, 1949.

LAWSON, J. G. *Deeper Experiences of Famous Christians.* Anderson: Gospel Trumpet Co., 1911.

LINCICOME, F. *Three D's of the Sanctified.* Winona Lake: Light and Life Press, 1932.

PACHE, RENE. *The Person and Work of the Holy Spirit.* Chicago: Moody Press, 1954.

PEARSE, M. G. *The Christianity of Jesus Christ.* New York: Eaton and Mains, undated.

PECK, J. T. *The Central Idea of Christianity.* Chicago: Chesbro, 1902.

ROGERS, HESTER ANN. *Life and Journal.* Cincinnati: Revivalist Press.

SHEPHERD, W. E. *Wrested Scriptures Made Plain.* Louisville: Pentecostal Publishing Co., 1900.

SMITH, WM. M. *The Backslider's Return.* Westfield: The Gospel Minister, 1955.

TAYLOR, J. PAUL. *The Music of Pentecost.* Winona Lake: Light and Life Press, 1945.

TAYLOR, R. S. *A Right Conception of Sin.* Kansas City: Beacon Hill Press, 1953.

TENNEY, MARY A. *Blueprint for a Christian World.* Winona Lake: Light and Life Press, 1953.

THEISSEN, H. C. *Lectures in Systematic Theology.* Grand Rapids: Wm. B. Eerdmans, 1951.

TORREY, R. A. *Baptism with the Holy Spirit.* Chicago: Moody Press.

TURNER, G. A. *The More Excellent Way.* Winona Lake: Light and Life Press, 1952.

WATSON, G. D. *Love Abounding.* Cincinnati: Revivalist Press, 1891.

WESLEY, JOHN. *Sermons,* Vol. I. New York: Soule and Mason, 1818.

WISEMAN, PETER. *Biblical Perfection.* London: Butler and Tanner Ltd., undated.

WRIGHT, J. STAFFORD. *Man in the Process of Time.* Grand Rapids: Wm. B. Eerdmans, 1956.